STUDY GUIDE

HENRY BORNE

SOCIETY

THE BASICS

FIFTH EDITION

JOHN J. MACIONIS

Kenyon College

PRENTICE HALL, Upper Saddle River, NJ 07458

©2000 by PRENTICE-HALL, INC.
Upper Saddle River, New Jersey 07458

10 9 8 7 6 5 4 3 2

ISBN 0-13-021123-0

Printed in the United States of America

Contents

Preface

This Study Guide has been written to enhance the foundation of sociological ideas and issues that are presented in the text *Society: The Basics (fifth edition)* by John Macionis. To help you review and think about the material found in the text, the Study Guide has been organized into several sections to accompany each chapter in the text.

A *Chapter Outline* provides a basis for organizing segments of information from each chapter in the text. A section on *Learning Objectives* identified the basic knowledge, explanations, comparisons, and understandings students should have after reading and studying each chapter in the text. This is followed by a section entitled *Key Terms* in which the important concepts from each chapter are listed, with space provided for you to write out the definition for each of the terms. Next, there is a section called *Important Researchers*. Researchers cited in the text are listed, with space provided for you to write significant ideas, findings, etc. for each researcher. The next section provides *Study Questions*, including true-false, multiple-choice, matching, fill-in, and definition and short-answer type questions. The study questions are followed by a section that provides *Answers to Study Questions*, including a listing of page numbers where the answers to these questions can be found. The seventh section entitled *In Focus—Important Issues*, provides an opportunity for you review ad summarize some of the important concepts and ideas presented in the chapter. The final section, *Analysis and Comment*, provides space for you to raise questions and make comments on the *boxes* presented in the text.

This Study Guide is intended to be a learning tool to accompany the text *Society: The Basics* (fifth edition). It hopefully will provide you with opportunities to more deeply benefit from the knowledge of sociology which the author of the text offers.

On a personal note, I want to once again congratulate John Macionis for writing another excellent introductory sociology text. He offers students a very meaningful perspective on many important sociological concepts, ideas, researchers, and issues. I believe students will be both challenged and excited by Dr. Macionis' text. I would like to thank Nancy Roberts, Sharon Chambliss, and Allison Westlake for all their wonderful efforts on this project. Their expertise and energy are so vital to the success of texts and supplements produced at Prentice Hall. I also want to thank the proofreaders who did such great work on this project. To my family--Cindy, Benjamin, and Abigail--thanks again for your patience and support!

1 Sociology: Perspective, Theory, and Method

PART I: CHAPTER OUTLINE

I. The Sociological Perspective
    A. Seeing the General in the Particular
    B. Seeing the Strange in the Familiar
    C. Seeing Individuality in Social Context
    D. Benefits of the Sociological Perspective
    E. Applied Sociology
    F. The Importance of Global Perspective

II. The Origins of Sociology
    A. Science and Sociology
    B. Social Change and Sociology
    C. Marginal Voices

III. Sociological Theory
    A. The Structural-Functional Paradigm
    B. The Social-Conflict Paradigm
    C. The Symbolic-Interaction Paradigm

IV. Scientific Sociology
    A. Concepts, Variables, and Measurement
    B. Correlation and Cause
    C. The Ideal of Objectivity
    D. Research and Gender
    E. Feminist Research
    F. Research Ethics

V. Research Methods
    A. Testing a Hypothesis: The Experiment
    B. Asking Questions: The Survey
    C. In the Field: Participant Observation
    D. The Second Time Around: Existing Sources
    E. Putting It All Together: Ten Steps in Sociological Research

VI. Summary

VIII. Key Concepts

VIII. Critical-Thinking Questions

XI. Learning Exercises

PART II: LEARNING OBJECTIVES

1. To be able to define sociology and understand the basic components of the sociological perspective.
2. To be able to provide examples of the ways in which social forces affect our everyday lives.
3. To recognize the importance of taking a global perspective in order to recognize the interdependence of our world's nations and people.
4. To be able to recognize the benefits of using the sociological perspective.
5. To be able to identify important historical factors in the development of the discipline of sociology as a science.
6. To be able to identify and discuss the differences between the three major theoretical paradigms used by sociologists in the analysis of society.
7. To understand the difference between sociology as a science and common sense.
8. To become familiar with the basic elements of science and how they are used in sociological investigation.
9. To develop an understanding about the difference between correlation and cause.
10. To recognize the difficulties in maintaining objectivity in sociological research.
11. To begin to view ethical considerations involved in studying people.
12. To become familiar with research methods used by sociologists in the investigation of society.
13. To be able to identify and describe each of the ten steps in sociological research.

PART III: KEY CONCEPTS

Define each of the following concepts in the space provided or on separate paper. Check the accuracy of your answers by referring to the key concepts section at the end of the chapter in the text as well as referring to italicized definitions located throughout the chapter. Do the same for each chapter as you read through the text during the semester.

Perspective and Theory

generalization
high-income countries
latent functions
low-income countries
macro-level orientation
manifest functions
metaphysical stage
micro-level orientation
middle-income countries
positivism
social-conflict paradigm
social dysfunction
social function
social marginality
social structure

sociology
stereotype
structural-functional paradigm
symbolic-interaction paradigm
theological stage
theoretical paradigm
theory

Methods

androcentricity
cause and effect
concept
correlation
dependent variable
empirical evidence
experiment
hypothesis
independent variable
interview
mean
measurement
median
mode
objectivity
operationalize
participant observation
population
questionnaire
reliability
research method
sample
science
spurious
survey
validity
variable

PART IV: IMPORTANT RESEARCHERS

Jane Addams   C.Wright Mills

Emile Durkheim   Karl Marx

Max Weber   Robert Merton

Peter Berger   Harriet Martineau

W.E.B. Du Bois   Auguste Comte

PART V: STUDY QUESTIONS

True-False

1.   T   F   A major component of the sociological perspective is the attempt to seek the *particular in the general*.
2.   T   F   Emile Durkheim's research on *suicide* illustrates the point that not all aspects of social life can be meaningfully studied using the sociological perspective.
3.   T   F   Protestants and Catholics, men and women, the married and unmarried have different suicide rates. Emile Durkheim explained these differences in terms of *social integration*.
4.   T   F   African Americans and females have *higher suicide rates* than whites and males.
5.   T   F   The *middle-income countries* of the world are primarily found in Latin America, Eastern Europe, and the former Soviet Union.

6.	T	F	The discipline of *sociology* first emerged in Europe during the nineteenth century.
7.	T	F	*Positivism* is an approach to understanding the world based on science.
8.	T	F	Jane Addams founded *Hill House*, a settlement house in Chicago, where she provided assistance to immigrant families.
9.	T	F	A *theory* is a statement of how and why specific facts are related.
10.	T	F	*Latent functions* refer to social processes which appear on the surface to be functional for society, but which are actually detrimental.
11.	T	F	The *symbolic-interaction* and *social-conflict* paradigms both operate from a *micro-level orientation*.
12.	T	F	Our author argues that a major strength of sociology is that it is basically just using *common sense*.
13.	T	F	A *concept* is defined as the process of determining the value of a variable in a specific case.
14.	T	F	The *mode* is the statistical term referring to the value which occurs most often in a series of numbers.
15.	T	F	*Reliability* refers to consistency in measurement.
16.	T	F	If two variables are *correlated*, by definition one is an *independent variable* and one is a *dependent variable*.
17.	T	F	A *hypothesis* is an unverified statement of a relationship between variables.
18.	T	F	A *sample* refers to a research method in which subjects respond to a series of items in a questionnaire or interview.
19.	T	F	The first step in the scientific research process should always be to determine what *research design* will be used to obtain data.
20.	T	F	A *generalization* is defined as an exaggerated description that one applies to all people in some category.

Multiple Choice

1. What is the *essential wisdom* of sociology?

   (a) Patterns in life are predestined.
   (b) Society is essentially non-patterned.
   (c) Surrounding society affects our actions, thoughts, and feelings.
   (d) Common sense needs to guide sociological investigations.

2. The sociological perspective involves *seeing the strange in the familiar*. Which of the following best provides the essential meaning of this phrase?

   (a) Sociology interprets social life primarily relying on common sense.
   (b) Sociologists believe intuition rather than logic is the preferred way to study society.
   (c) Sociologists focus on the bizarre behaviors that occur in society.
   (d) Sociologists work to avoid the assumption that human behavior is simply a matter of what people decide to do.

3. Which sociologist linked the incidence of *suicide* to the degree of *social integration* of different categories of people?

   (a) Emile Durkheim
   (b) Max Weber
   (c) Robert Merton
   (d) C. Wright Mills
   (e) Karl Marx

4. Which of the following is/are identified as situations that simulate *sociological thinking*?

   (a) social diversity
   (b) social marginality
   (c) social crisis
   (d) all of the above
   (e) none of the above

5. In that sociology has an impact on some public policy and also helps prepare people for the many different types of jobs illustrates the _____ nature of this field of study.

   (a) micro
   (b) applied
   (c) theoretical
   (d) secondary

6. The term *sociology* was coined in 1838 by:

   (a) Auguste Comte.
   (b) Karl Marx.
   (c) Herbert Spencer.
   (d) Emile Durkheim.
   (e) Max Weber.

7. According to Auguste Comte, the key to understanding society was to look at it:

   (a) using common sense.
   (b) using intuition.
   (c) theologically.
   (d) metaphysically.
   (e) scientifically.

8. *Positivism* is the idea that _____, rather than any other type of human understanding, is the path to knowledge.

  (a) human nature
  (b) science
  (c) faith
  (d) optimism
  (e) common sense

9. Two *founders of sociology* who had radically different views on society--one more traditional and conservative, the other more critical and focused on change--were:

  (a) C. Wright Mills and Robert Merton.
  (b) Jane Addams and Peter Blau.
  (c) Emile Durkheim and Robert Merton.
  (d) Auguste Comte and Karl Marx.
  (e) Karl Marx and C. Wright Mills.

10. A set of fundamental assumptions that guides thinking and research is the definition for:

  (a) a theoretical paradigm.
  (b) manifest functions.
  (c) social marginality.
  (d) positivism.

11. Consequences of social structure which are largely *unrecognized* and *unintended* are called:

  (a) paradigms.
  (b) manifest functions.
  (c) latent functions.
  (d) social integration.
  (e) social marginality.

12. Which of the following theoretical perspectives is best suited for analysis using a *macro-level* orientation?

  (a) dramaturgical analysis
  (b) social exchange theory
  (c) symbolic-interactionist paradigm
  (d) ethnomethodology
  (e) social-conflict paradigm

13. The questions--How is society experienced? and, how do individuals attempt to shape the reality perceived by others? are most likely asked by a researcher using which of the following theoretical paradigms?

    (a) structural-functional
    (b) symbolic-interaction
    (c) social Darwinism
    (d) social-conflict
    (e) none of the above

14. _____ *evidence* is information we can verify with our senses.

    (a) Consensual
    (b) Common sense
    (c) Intrapsychic
    (d) Holistic
    (e) Empirical

15. _____ is a logical system that bases knowledge on direct, systematic observation.

    (a) Research method
    (b) Sociological Investigation
    (c) Hypothesis
    (d) Science
    (e) Theory

16. Which of the following common sense statements are *false* according to empirical evidence?

    (a) Differences in social behavior of women and men reflect "human nature."
    (b) The United States is a middle-class society where most people are more or less equal.
    (c) People marry because they are in love.
    (d) All of the above
    (e) None of the above

17. Which of the following aspects of social life is used by the author to illustrate the insights provided by the theoretical paradigms used by sociologists?

    (a) sports
    (b) war
    (c) bureaucracy
    (d) education
    (e) family

18. A _____ is a mental construct that represents some part of the world, inevitably in a simplified form.

   (a) variable
   (b) concept
   (c) hypothesis
   (d) research design
   (e) measurement

19. Specifying exactly what is to be measured in assigning a value to a variable is called:

   (a) validity.
   (b) objectivity.
   (c) operationalizing a variable.
   (d) reliability.
   (e) control.

20. The *arithmetic average* in a series of numbers is the:

   (a) control.
   (b) median.
   (c) mode.
   (d) mean.
   (e) conceptualization.

21. The *descriptive statistic* that represents the value that occurs *midway* in a series of numbers is called the:

   (a) median.
   (b) correlation.
   (c) mode.
   (d) norm.
   (e) mean.

22. The quality of *consistency* in measurement is known as:

   (a) spuriousness.
   (b) reliability.
   (c) empirical evidence.
   (d) objectivity.
   (e) validity.

23. Measuring what one *intends* to measure is the quality of measurement known as:

  (a) reliability.
  (b) operationalization.
  (c) validity.
  (d) control.
  (e) objectivity.

24. A higher level of education causes greater earnings over one's lifetime. In this case, *higher level of education* is:

  (a) a spurious variable.
  (b) a dependent variable.
  (c) an independent variable.
  (d) the median.
  (e) the control variable.

25. A state of personal neutrality in conducting research is known as:

  (a) subjective interpretation.
  (b) objectivity.
  (c) control variable.
  (d) spurious relationship.
  (e) validity.

26. According to Max Weber, it is essential that researchers be _____ in their investigations.

  (a) value-free
  (b) subjective
  (c) spurious
  (d) selective in their reporting of facts
  (e) concerned about social welfare

27. The issue of *androcentricity* relates to:

  (a) over-generalization.
  (b) social activism.
  (c) economic elitism.
  (d) gender bias.
  (e) political correctness.

28. An unverified statement of a relationship between variables is a(n):

    (a)   correlation.
    (b)   logical deduction.
    (c)   hypothesis.
    (d)   logical induction.
    (e)   theory.

29. A systematic plan for conducting research is the definition for:

    (a)   theory.
    (b)   hypothesis.
    (c)   operationalizing a variable.
    (d)   sample.
    (e)   research method.

30. Which *research method* is explanatory and is usually used to test hypotheses?

    (a)   the survey
    (b)   participant observation
    (c)   the experiment
    (d)   the use of existing sources
    (e)   the interview

31. A disadvantage of the *interview* type of survey is that:

    (a)   it does not permit follow-up questions.
    (b)   the subjects' answers cannot be clarified.
    (c)   a person is less likely to complete a survey if contacted personally.

32. Sociology is not involved in *stereotyping* because:

    (a)   Sociologists do not indiscriminately apply any generalization to all individuals.
    (b)   Sociologists base their generalizations on research.
    (c)   Sociologists strive to be fair-minded.
    (d)   all of the above.
    (e)   none of the above.

33. The question representing the *fifth step* in the sociological research process is:

    (a)   How will you record the data?
    (b)   Are there ethical concerns?
    (c)   What have others already learned?
    (d)   What do the data tell you?
    (e)   What are your conclusions?

Matching

Perspective and Theory

1. ____ The study of the larger world and our society's place in it.
2. ____ Nations with limited industrialization and moderate personal income.
3. ____ Used the Great Depression to illustrate the importance of social crisis as a prompt to view the world sociologically.
4. ____ An approach to studying the world based on science.
5. ____ A statement of how and why specific facts are related.
6. ____ A framework for building theory based on the assumption that society is a complex system whose parts work together to promote solidarity and stability.
7. ____ Relatively stable patterns of social behavior.
8. ____ The largely unrecognized and unintended consequences of social structure.
9. ____ A framework for building theory that sees society as an arena of inequality that generates conflict and change.
10. ____ An exaggerated description applied to all people in some category.

a.	common sense	i.	global perspective
b.	theory	j.	social structure
c.	social-conflict paradigm	k.	C. Wright Mills
d.	Third-World nations	l.	positivism
e.	Herbert Spencer	m.	structural-functional paradigm
f.	sociological imagination	n.	generalization
g.	middle-income countries	o.	sociology
h.	latent functions	p.	stereotype

Methods

1. ____ A logical system that bases knowledge on direct, systematic observation.
2. ____ A mental construct that represents an aspect of the world, inevitably in a somewhat simplified way.
3. ____ The quality of measurement gained by measuring precisely what one intends to measure.
4. ____ A relationship in which two (or more) variables change together.
5. ____ An apparent, although false, relationship between two (or more) variables caused by some other variable.
6. ____ A state of personal neutrality in conducting research.
7. ____ A research method in which subjects respond to a series of statements and questions in a questionnaire of interview.
8. ____ A part of a population that represents the whole.
9. ____ Fieldwork by cultural anthropologists is an example of this type of research.
10. ____ A research method in which a researcher uses data collected by others.

Fill-In

1. The scientific study of human social activity is the general definition for _____.

2. Emile Durkheim reasoned that the variation in *suicide rates* between different categories of people had to do with *social* _____.

3. A _____ _____ is the study of the larger world and our society's place in it.

4. The United States, Canada, and most of the nations of Western Europe are classified in terms of economic development as being the _____-income countries.

5. Three important reasons for taking a *global perspective* include: societies around the world are increasingly _____, many human problems that we face in the United States are far more _____ elsewhere, and it is a good way to learn more about _____.

6. Auguste Comte asserted that scientific sociology was a result of a progression throughout history of thought and understanding in *three stages*: the _____, _____, and _____.

7. The development of sociology as an academic discipline was shaped within the context of three revolutionary changes in Europe during the seventeenth and eighteenth centuries. These included *a new* _____ _____, the *growth of* _____, and _____ *change*.

8. A _____ is a statement of how and why specific facts are related.

9. A _____ _____ provides a basic image of society that guides thinking and research.

10. Concern with small-scale patterns of social interaction, such as *symbolic-interaction theory*. operates through a _____-_____ *orientation*.

11. _____ *evidence* refers to information we can verify with our senses.

12. _____ is a procedure for determining the value of a variable in a specific case.

13. _____ refers to two variables that *vary together,* such as number of years of education and earned income.

14. The state of *personal neutrality* in conducting research is referred to as _____.

15. The German sociologist _____ _____ distinguished between *value-relevant* choice of research and *value-free* conduct of scientific investigation.

16. Criticisms concerning Max Weber's *value-free* research are that researchers must always _____ their data and all research is _____.

17. Five ways in which *gender* can jeopardize good research include: _____, _____, _____, gender _____, _____ standards, and _____.

18. The _____ is a *research model* in which subjects respond to a series of statements or questions in a *questionnaire* or an *interview*.
19. A _____ is a part of a population that represents the whole.
20. Two types of surveys include _____ and _____.
21. A _____ is an exaggerated description applied to all people in some category.

Definition and Short-Answer

1. Differentiate between the concepts *manifest* and *latent functions* and provide an illustration for each.
2. Discuss Emile Durkheim's explanation of how *suicide rates* vary between different categories of people. Explain how this research demonstrates the application of the *sociological perspective*.
3. What are the three types of countries identified in the text as measured by their level of *economic development*? What are the characteristics of the countries that represent each of the three types?
4. What are the three major reasons why a *global perspective* is so important today?
5. What were three *social changes* in seventeenth and eighteenth century Europe that provided the context for the development of *sociology* as a scientific discipline?
6. What are the three major components of the *sociological perspective*? Describe and provide an illustration for each.
7. What are the three major *theoretical paradigms* used by sociologists? Identify two key questions raised by each in the analysis of society. Identify one weakness for each of these paradigms for understanding the nature of human social life.
8. How do the three theoretical paradigms help us understand the place of *spots* in our society?
9. What are three reasons why sociology is *not to be considered* nothing more than *stereotyping*?
10. What are four *benefits* of using the sociological perspective?
11. What is the relationship between *sociology* and *social marginality*? Provide an illustration.
12. What are the three factors which must be determined to conclude that a *cause and effect* relationship between two variables may exist?
13. Margaret Eichler points out five dangers to sound research that involves *gender*. Identify and define each.
14. Define the concept *hypothesis*. Further, write your own hypothesis and operationalize the variables identified.
15. Identify two advantages and two disadvantages for each of the four major *research methods* used by sociologists.
16. What are the basic steps of the sociological *research process*? Briefly describe each.
17. Three illustrations are provided to show that *common sense* does not always guide us to a meaningful sense of reality. What two examples can you give concerning common sense not paving the way toward our understanding of what is really happening in social life?
18. Identify and define the *major elements* of scientific investigation.
19. Using standardized high school achievements tests as an example, illustrate the difference between *reliability* and *validity*.
20. What are the basic guidelines for *research ethics* in sociological research?

PART VI: ANSWERS TO STUDY QUESTIONS

True-False

1.	F	(p. 2)	11.	F	(p. 14)
2.	F	(p. 3)	12.	F	(p. 15)
3.	T	(p. 3)	13.	F	(p. 16)
4.	F	(p. 5)	14.	T	(p. 18)
5.	T	(p. 6)	15.	T	(p. 18)
6.	T	(p. 8)	16.	F	(p. 18)
7.	T	(p. 9)	17.	T	(p. 22)
8.	T	(p. 10)	18.	F	(p. 22)
9.	T	(p. 11)	19.	F	(p. 24)
10.	F	(p. 12)	20.	F	(p. 24)

Multiple Choice

1.	c	(p. 2)	18	b	(p. 16)
2.	d	(p. 3)	19.	c	(p. 17)
3.	a	(p. 3)	20.	d	(p. 18)
4.	d	(p. 4)	21.	a	(p. 18)
5.	b	(p. 5)	22.	b	(p. 18)
6.	a	(p. 8)	23.	c	(p. 18)
7.	e	(p. 9)	24.	b	(p. 18)
8.	b	(p. 9)	25.	b	(p. 19)
9.	d	(p. 10)	26.	a	(p. 19)
10.	a	(p. 11)	27.	d	(p. 19)
11.	c	(p. 12)	28.	c	(p. 22)
12.	e	(p. 14)	29.	e	(p. 22)
13.	b	(p. 15)	30.	c	(p. 22)
14.	e	(p. 15)	31.	d	(p. 22)
15.	d	(p. 15)	32.	d	(p. 24)
16.	d	(p. 15-16)	33.	b	(p. 25)
17.	a	(p. 16)			

Matching

Perspective and Theory:

1.	i	(p. 6)	6.	m	(p. 11)
2.	g	(p. 6)	7.	j	(p. 6)
3.	k	(p. 4)	8.	h	(p. 12)
4.	l	(p. 9)	9.	c	(p. 13)
5.	b	(p. 11)	10.	p	(p. 24)

Methods:

1.	j	(p. 15)	6.	b	(p. 19)
2.	d	(p. 19)	7.	a	(p. 22)
3.	h	(p. 18)	8.	e	(p 22)
4.	g	(p. 18)	9.	c	(p. 22)
5.	i	(p. 19)	10.	f	(p. 23)

Fill-In

1. sociology (p. 2)
2. integration (p. 3)
3. global perspective (p. 6)
4. high (p. 6)
5. interconnected, serious, ourselves (p. 8)
6. theological, metaphysical, scientific (p. 9)
7. industrial economy, cities, political (p. 10)
8. theory (p. 11)
9. theoretical paradigm (p. 11)
10. micro-level (p. 14)
11. Empirical (p. 15)
12. Measurement (p. 17)
13. Correlation (p. 18)
14. Objectivity (p. 19)
15. Max Weber (p. 19)
16. Interpret, political (p. 19)
17. Androcentricity, overgeneralizing, blindness, double, interference (pp. 19-20)
18. survey (p. 22)
19. sample (p. 22)
20. questionnaires, interviews (p. 22)
21. stereotype (p. 24)

PART VII: IN FOCUS--MAJOR ISSUES

- Illustrate each of the following major components of the *sociological perspective:*

  Seeing the general in the particular:

  Seeing the strange in the familiar:

  Seeing individuality in social context:

- What are the three *benefits of the sociological perspective?*

- What are three reasons why *global perspective* is so important today?

- Identify the major concepts and dominant viewpoint for each of the following *theoretical paradigms:*

  Structural-Functional

  Social-Conflict

  Symbolic-Interaction

- Briefly describe each of the following *research resigns* used by sociologists:

  Experiment

  Survey

  Participant Observation

  Existing Sources

- What three factors need to be known to be sure *cause-and-effect* exists?

PART VIII: ANALYSIS AND COMMENT

Go back through the chapter and write down key points from each of the following boxes. Then, for each of the boxes identified, write out three questions concerning the issues raised which you feel would be valuable to discuss in class. Do the same for each chapter as you read through the text.

Social Diversity

"What's in a Name? How Social Forces Affect Personal Choice"

Key Points: Questions:

Critical Thinking

"Sports: Playing the Theory Game"

Key Points: Questions:

Controversy and Debate

"Is Sociology Nothing More than Stereotypes?"

Key Points: Questions:

Window on the World--Global Map 1-1

"Economic Development in Global Perspective"

Key Points: Questions:

Seeing Ourselves--National Map 1-1

"Suicide Rates Across the United States"

Key Points: Questions:

2 Culture

PART I: CHAPTER OUTLINE

    I.   What is Culture?
          A.   Culture and Human Intelligence
    II.   The Components of Culture
          A.   Symbols
          B.   Language
          C.   Values
          D.   Norms
          E.   "Ideal" and "Real" Culture
    III.   Technology and Culture
          A.   Hunting and Gathering
          B.   Horticulture and Pastoralism
          C.   Agriculture
          D.   Industry
          E.   Postindustrial Information Technology
    IV.   Cultural Diversity
          A.   High Culture and Popular Culture
          B.   Subculture
          C.   Multiculturalism
          D.   Counterculture
          E.   Cultural Change
          F.   Ethnocentrism and Cultural Relativity
          G.   A Global Culture?
    V.   Theoretical Analysis of Culture
          A.   Structural-Functional Analysis
          B.   Social-Conflict Analysis
          C.   Sociobiology
    VI.   Culture and Human Freedom
    VII. Summary
    VIII. Key Concepts
    IX.   Critical-Thinking Questions
    X.   Learning Exercises

PART II: LEARNING OBJECTIVES

1.   To begin to understand the sociological meaning of the concept of culture.
2.   To consider the relationship between human intelligence and culture.

3.   To know the components of culture and to be able to provide examples of each.
4.   To consider the current state of knowledge about whether language is uniquely human.
5.   To consider the significance of symbols in the construction and maintenance of social reality.
6.   To identify the dominant values in our society and to recognize their interrelationships with one another and with other aspects of our culture.
7.   To be able to provide examples of the different types of norms operative in a culture, and how these are related to the process of social control.
8.   To be able to identify and describe the different types of societies as distinguished by their level of technology.
9.   To be able to explain how subcultures and countercultures contribute to cultural diversity.
10.   To begin to develop your understanding of multiculturalism.
11.   To be able to differentiate between ethnocentrism and cultural relativism.
12.   To be able to compare and contrast analyses of culture using structural-functional, social-conflict, and sociobiological paradigms.
13.   To be able to identify the consequences of culture for human freedom and constraint.

PART III: KEY CONCEPTS

Afrocentrism
beliefs
agriculture
counterculture
cultural conflict
cultural ecology
cultural integration
cultural lag
cultural relativism
cultural transmission
cultural universals
culture
culture shock
discovery
diffusion
ethnocentrism
Eurocentrism
folkways
high culture
horticulture
ideal culture
idealism
industry
instincts
invention
language
material culture

materialism
multiculturalism
natural selection
nonmaterial culture
norms
pastoralism
popular culture
postindustrial
real culture
Sapir-Whorf thesis
society
sociobiology
sociocultural evolution
subculture
symbol
technology
values

PART IV: IMPORTANT RESEARCHERS

Napoleon Chagnon

Edward Sapir and Benjamin Whorf

Marvin Harris

Robin Williams

PART V: STUDY QUESTIONS

True-False

1.	T	F	*Individualism* is even more valued in Japan than in the United States.
2.	T	F	According to the evolutionary record, the human line diverged from our closest primate relative, the great apes, some *12 millions years ago*.
3.	T	F	Only humans rely on *culture* rather than *instinct* to ensure the survival of their kind..
4.	T	F	Cultural *symbols* often change over time, and even vary within a single society.
5.	T	F	*Cultural transmission* is defined as the process by which one generation passes on culture to the next.
6.	T	F	The *Sapir-Whorf thesis* concerns the extent to which the dominant values of a culture are affected by its level of technological development.

7.	T	F	*Values* are defined as rules and expectations by which society guides the behavior of its members.
8.	T	F	*Mores* are norms which have little moral significance within a culture.
9.	T	F	*Horticulture* refers to the use of hand-tools to raise crops.
10.	T	F	*Hunting and gathering societies* tend to be characterized by more social inequality than horticultural or agrarian societies.
11.	T	F	*Agrarian societies* emerged about 5,000 years ago.
12.	T	F	During the last decade, most *immigrants* to the United States have come from Asia and Latin America.
13.	T	F	Compared to Japan, the United States is a very *monocultural* nation.
14.	T	F	*Subcultures* involve not just differences but hierarchy.
15.	T	F	Three major sources of cultural change are *invention, discovery,* and *diffusion.*
16.	T	F	The practice of judging any culture by its own standards is referred to as *ethnocentrism.*
17.	T	F	*Structural-functionalists* argue that there are no *cultural universals.*
18.	T	F	According to the author of our text, culture has diminished human autonomy to the point where we are *culturally programmed* much like other animals are *genetically programmed.*

Multiple-Choice

1. The *Mohegans* are a tribal group living in:

    (a) South America.
    (b) North America.
    (c) Asia.
    (d) Africa.
    (e) Central America.

2. *Culture* is:

    (a) the process by which members of a culture encourage conformity to social norms.
    (b) the beliefs, values, behavior, and material objects that constitute a people's way of life.
    (c) the practice of judging another society's norms.
    (d) a group of people who engage in interaction with one another on a continuous basis.
    (e) the aspects of social life people admire most.

3. The personal disorientation that accompanies exposure to an unfamiliar way of life is termed:

    (a) anomie.
    (b) alienation.
    (c) cultural relativism.
    (d) culture shock.
    (e) cultural transmission.

4. The organized interaction of people in a nation or within some other boundary is the definition for:

    (a)   culture.
    (b)   social structure.
    (c)   society.
    (d)   socialization.
    (e)   acculturation.

5. The *Yanomamo* are:

    (a)   a small tribal group of herders living in Eastern Africa.
    (b)   a technologically primitive horticultural society living in South America.
    (c)   a nomadic culture living above the Arctic circle as hunters.
    (d)   a small, dying society living as farmers in a mountainous region of western Africa.
    (e)   a people who until very recently were living in complete isolation from the rest of the world in a tropical rain forest in Malaysia.

6. Studying *fossil records*, scientists have concluded that the first creatures with clearly human characteristics existed about _____ years ago.

    (a)   3 million
    (b)   12 thousand
    (c)   40 million
    (d)   60 thousand
    (e)   12 million

7. *Homo sapiens* is a Latin term that means:

    (a)   thinking person.
    (b)   to walk upright.
    (c)   evolving life form.
    (d)   dependent person.

8. Which of the following identifies two of the *components of culture*?

    (a)   values and norms
    (b)   social change and social statics
    (c)   social structure and social function
    (d)   people and the natural environment

9. *Symbols*, a component of culture, can:

    (a)   vary from culture to culture.
    (b)   provide a foundation for the reality we experience.
    (c)   vary within a given culture.
    (d)   all of the above

10. A system of *symbols* that allows members of a society to communicate with one other is the definition of:

    (a)   language.
    (b)   cultural relativity.
    (c)   cultural transmission.
    (d)   values.
    (e)   norms.

11. Culturally defined *standards* of desirability, goodness, and beauty, which serve as broad guidelines for social living, is the definition for:

    (a)   norms.
    (b)   mores.
    (c)   beliefs.
    (d)   sanctions.
    (e)   values.

12. The *Sapir-Whorf thesis* relates to:

    (a)   human evolution.
    (b)   language and cultural relativity.
    (c)   social sanctions.
    (d)   victimization patterns.

13. _____ is a system of symbols that allow people to communicate with one another.

    (a)   Values
    (b)   Language
    (c)   Norms
    (d)   Sanctions
    (e)   Beliefs

14. The process by which one generation passes culture on to the next refers to:

    (a) cultural transmission.
    (b) Sociocultural evolution.
    (c) Cultural relativism.
    (d) Ethnocentrism.

15. Rules and expectations by which a society guides the behavior of is members refers to:

    (a) norms.
    (b) values.
    (c) sanctions.
    (d) beliefs.

16. The old adage "Do as I say, not as I do" illustrates the distinction between:

    (a) folkways and mores.
    (b) the Sapir-Whorf hypothesis.
    (c) cultural integration and cultural lag.
    (d) ideal and real culture.
    (e) subcultures and countercultures.

17. *Tangible* human creations are called:

    (a) technology.
    (b) values.
    (c) artifacts.
    (d) real culture.

18. Gerhard and Jean Lenski focus on which factor as a major determinant of social change?

    (a) human ideas
    (b) technology
    (c) social solidarity
    (d) religious doctrine

19. The concept of *sociocultural evolution* focuses our attention on _____ as a key in cultural change?

    (a) technology
    (b) values
    (c) beliefs
    (d) sanctions

20. A settlement of several hundred people who use hand tools to cultivate plants, is family-centered, and came into existence 10-12,000 years ago is a(n):

    (a)   hunting and gathering society.
    (b)   horticultural society.
    (c)   pastoral society.
    (d)   agrarian society.

21. The key organizational principle of *hunting and gathering* societies is:

    (a)   government.
    (b)   religion.
    (c)   health.
    (d)   kinship.

22. Which of the following qualities is/are more characteristic of *horticultural* and *agrarian* societies as compared to hunting and gathering societies?

    (a)   greater social inequality
    (b)   greater material surplus
    (c)   greater specialization
    (d)   all of the above

23. *Agrarian societies* first emerged about _____ years ago.

    (a)   1,000
    (b)   12,000
    (c)   25,000
    (d)   50,000
    (e)   5,000

24. *Postindustrial society* is _____-based.

    (a)   family
    (b)   labor and work
    (c)   gender
    (d)   leisure
    (e)   idea and information

25. Cultural patterns that set apart some segment of a society's population is termed:

    (a) social stratification.
    (b) social differentiation.
    (c) counterculture.
    (d) cultural lag.
    (e) subculture.

26. Cultural patterns that distinguish some segment of a society's population is termed:

    (a) social stratification.
    (b) counterculture.
    (c) culture shock.
    (d) cultural lag.
    (e) subculture.

27. Which of the following statements is most accurate concerning responses to a survey by students entering college, 1968 and 1998?

    (a) Students today are far more likely to want to develop a philosophy of life.
    (b) Students today are far more likely to want to keep up with political affairs.
    (c) Students today are far more likely to want to help other in difficulty.
    (d) Students today are more likely to want to well off financially.

28. Inconsistencies within a cultural system resulting from the unequal rates at which different cultural elements change is termed:

    (a) cultural lag.
    (b) counterculture.
    (c) culture shock.
    (d) cultural relativity.
    (e) ethnocentrism.

29. The spread of cultural elements from one society to another is called:

    (a) invention.
    (b) integration.
    (c) diffusion.
    (d) discovery.

30. *Ethnocentrism* is:

   (a)   an educational program recognizing past and present cultural diversity.
   (b)   cultural patterns that set apart some segment of society's population.
   (c)   cultural patterns that strongly oppose those widely accepted within a society.
   (d)   the practice of judging another culture by the standards of one's own culture.
   (e)   the practice of judging another culture by its own standards.

31. The theoretical paradigm that focuses upon *universal cultural traits* is:

   (a)   cultural ecology.
   (b)   structural-functionalism.
   (c)   cultural materialism.
   (d)   social-conflict.

32. The philosophical doctrine of *materialism* is utilized in the analysis of culture by proponents of which theoretical paradigm?

   (a)   sociobiologists
   (b)   cultural ecology
   (c)   social-conflict
   (d)   structural-functionalism

33. Political differences, often expressed hostility, based on disagreement over cultural values refers to:

   (a)   cultural conflict.
   (b)   social chaos.
   (c)   cultural materialism.
   (d)   cultural shock.

Matching

1.   ____   The intangible world of ideas created by members of society.
2.   ____   Anything that carries a particular meaning recognized by people who share a culture.
3.   ____   The official language of twenty percent of the world's population.
4.   ____   States that people perceive the world through the cultural lens of language.
5.   ____   Rules and expectations by which a society guides the behavior of its members.
6.   ____   The use of hand tools to raise crops.
7.   ____   Knowledge that a people apply to the task of living in their surroundings.
8.   ____   An educational program recognizing past and present diversity in U.S. society and promoting the equality of all cultural traditions.
9.   ____   Cultural patterns that strongly oppose those widely accepted within a society.
10. ____   The fact that cultural elements change at different rates, which may disrupt a cultural system.
11. ____   The practice of judging another culture by the standards of one's own culture.
12. ____   A theoretical paradigm that explores ways in which biology affects how humans create culture.

a.	horticulture	i.	Chinese
b.	sociobiology	j.	technology
c.	counterculture	k.	norms
d.	cultural lag	l.	symbol
e.	Sapir-Whorf thesis	m.	mores
f.	ethnocentrism	n.	English
g.	nonmaterial culture	o.	agriculture
h.	multiculturalism		

Fill-In

1. The 6 billion people on earth today are members of a single biological species: _____.

2. _____ are the biological programming over which animals have no control.

3. The *tangible things* created by members of society are referred to as _____ _____.

4. The concept _____ _____ is derived from the Latin meaning *thinking person*.

5. Four key *components of culture* include: _____, _____, _____, and _____.

6. Anything that carries a particular meaning recognized by people who share culture refers to _____.

7. The process by which one generation passes culture to the next refers to _____ _____.

8. Specific statements that people hold to be true are _____.

9. Culture shock is both _____ and _____ by the traveler..

10. While _____ are culturally defined standards of desirability, goodness, and beauty that serve as broad guidelines for social living, _____ are specific statements that people hold to be true.

11. The most widely spoken languages in the world today, spoken by 20, 10, and 6 percent of the world's population respectively are _____, _____, and _____.

12. _____ are rules and expectations by which a society guides the behavior of its members.

13. _____ refers to knowledge that people apply to the task of living in their surroundings.

14. _____ refers to large-scale cultivation using plows harnessed to animals or more powerful energy sources.

15. _____ *culture* refers to cultural patterns widespread among a society's population.

16. _____ is an educational program recognizing the cultural diversity of the United States and promoting the equality of all cultural traditions.

17. The fact that some cultural elements change more quickly than others, which may disrupt a cultural system refers to _____ _____.

18. _____ refers to the practice of judging another culture by the standards of one's own culture.

19. The _____-_____ *paradigm* depicts culture as a complex strategy for meeting human needs. Borrowing from the philosophical doctrine of *idealism*, this approach views values at the core of culture.

20. *Social conflict theory* is rooted in the philosophical doctrine of _____ which holds that a society's system of material production has a powerful effect on the rest of culture.

21. _____ is a theoretical paradigm that studies the ways in which human biology affects the way we create culture.

Definition and Short-Answer

1. Three *causes of cultural change* are identified in the text. Identify these and provide an illustration of each.
2. Review the statistics presented in *Table 2-1* (p. 49) concerning changing values among college students. What have been the most significant changes? In which areas have values remained consistent? To what extent do your values fit the picture of contemporary college students? Explain.
3. What are the basic qualities of the *Yanomamo* culture? What factors do you think may explain why they are so aggressive? To what extent are you able to view these people from a *cultural relativistic perspective*?
4. What is the basic position being taken by *sociobiologists* concerning the nature of culture? What are three examples used by sociobiologists to argue that human culture is determined by biology? To what extent do you agree or disagree with their position? Explain.
5. What is the *Sapir-Whorf thesis*? What evidence supports it? What evidence is inconsistent with this hypothesis?
6. Write a paragraph in which you express your opinions about the issue of multiculturalism in our society. Address the benefits of this perspective being suggested by proponents of multiculturalism, as well as the potential problems with this perspective suggested by its critics.
7. How do the Lenski's define *sociocultural evolution*?
8. What are the basic *types of societies* based on level of technological development? What are three important characteristics of each type of society?
9. Provide two examples of how culture *constrains* us (limits our freedom).
10. Differentiate between *values* and *norms*, providing two illustrations for each.
11. Review the list of *core values* of our culture in the United States. Rank order the ten identified in the text in terms of how important they are in our society from your point of view. What values, if any, do you believe should be included in the "top ten" list? Do you feel any of those listed should not be on the list?

PART VI: ANSWERS TO STUDY QUESTIONS

True-False

1.	F	(p. 35)	10.	F	(p. 42)
2.	T	(p. 35)	11.	T	(p. 42)
3.	T	(p. 35)	12.	T	(p. 45)
4.	T	(p. 37)	13.	F	(p. 45)
5.	T	(p. 38)	14.	T	(p. 46)
6.	F	(p. 38)	15.	T	(p. 50)
7.	F	(p. 38)	16.	F	(p. 50)

| 8. | F | (p. 41) | 17. | F | (p. 53) |
| 9. | T | (p. 42) | 18. | F | (p. 56) |

Multiple Choice

1.	b	(p. 34)	18.	b	(p. 42)
2.	b	(p. 35)	19.	a	(p. 42)
3.	d	(p. 35)	20.	b	(p. 42)
4.	c	(p. 36)	21.	d	(p. 42)
5.	b	(p. 36)	22.	d	(p. 42)
6.	a	(p. 36)	23.	e	(p. 42)
7.	a	(p. 37)	24.	e	(p. 45)
8.	a	(p. 37)	25.	b	(p. 46)
9.	d	(p. 37)	26.	e	(p. 46)
10.	a	(p. 38)	27.	d	(p. 49)
11.	e	(p. 38)	28.	a	(p. 50)
12.	b	(p. 38)	29.	c	(p. 50)
13.	b	(p. 38)	30.	d	(p. 50)
14.	a	(p. 38)	31.	b	(p. 53)
15.	a	(p. 41)	32.	c	(p. 54)
16.	d	(p. 41)	33.	a	(p. 56)
17.	c	(p. 41)			

Matching

1.	g	(p. 35)	7.	j	(pp. 41-42)
2.	l	(p. 37)	8.	h	(p. 47)
3.	i	(p. 39)	9.	c	(p. 49)
4.	e	(p. 39)	10.	d	(p. 50)
5.	k	(p. 41)	11.	f	(p. 50)
6.	a	(p. 42)	12.	b	(p. 54)

Fill-In

1.	homo sapiens (p. 33)	13.	Technology (pp. 41-42)
2.	Instincts (p. 35)	14.	Agriculture (p. 42)
3.	material culture (p. 35)	15.	Popular (p. 46)
4.	homo sapiens (p. 37)	16.	Multiculturalism (p. 47)
5.	symbols, language, values, norms (p. 37)	17.	Cultural lag (p. 50)
		18.	Ethnocentrism (p. 50)
6.	symbol (p. 37)	19.	Structural-functionalism (p. 53)
7.	cultural transmission (p. 38)	20.	materialism (p. 54)
8.	beliefs (p. 38)	21.	Sociobiology (p. 54)

9. experienced, inflicted (pp. 37-38)23.
10. values, beliefs (p. 38)
11. Chinese, English, Spanish (p. 39)
12. Norms (p. 41)

PART VII: IN FOCUS—MAJOR ISSES

- Define and illustrate the concepts of *material* and *nonmaterial culture*.

- Define and illustrate each of the following four *components of nonmaterial culture*.

Symbols:

Language:

Values:

Norms:

- Identify and illustrate the ten *dominant U.S. values* listed in the text.

- Describe the major characteristics of societies operating at each of the following levels of *sociolcultural evolution.*

  Hunting and Gathering:

  Horticultural

  Pastoral

  Agricultural

  Industry

  Postindustrial

- Identify, define, and illustrate three examples of *cultural diversity.*

- What are three examples of evidence that a *global culture* exists?

- Briefly identify the basic arguments being made about culture by theorists using each of the following three *theoretical paradigms*.

Structural-Functional Paradigm

Social-Conflict Paradigm

Sociobiology

PART VIII: ANALYSIS AND COMMENT

Global Sociology

"Confronting the Yanomamo: The Experience of Culture Shock"

Key Points: Questions:

Exploring Cyber-Society

"Here Comes Virtual Culture"

Key Points: Questions:

Controversy and Debate

"What Are the Culture Wars?"

Key Points: Questions:

Window on the World--Global Map 2-1

"Language in Global Perspective"

Key Points: Questions:

Seeing Ourselves--National Map 2-1 and 2-2

"Who's Upper Crust? High Culture and Popular Culture across the United States"

Key Points: Questions:

3 | Socialization

PART I: CHAPTER OUTLINE

I. Social Experience: The Key to Our Humanity
- A. Human Development: Nature and Nurture
- B. Social Isolation

II. Understanding Socialization
- A. Sigmund Freud: The Elements of Personality
- B. Jean Piaget: Cognitive Development
- C. Lawrence Kohlberg: Moral Development
- D. Carol Gilligan: The Gender Factor
- E. George Herbert Mead: The Social Self
- F. Erik H. Erikson: Eight Stages of Development

III. Agents of Socialization
- A. The Family
- B. The School
- C. The Peer Group
- D. The Mass Media

IV. Socialization and the Life Course
- A. Childhood
- B. Adolescence
- C. Adulthood
- D. Old Age
- E. Death and Dying
- F. The Life Course: An Overview

V. Resocialization: Total Institutions

VI. Summary

VII. Key Concepts

VIII Learning Exercises

IX. Critical-Thinking Questions

PART II: LEARNING OBJECTIVES

1. To understand the "nature-nurture" debate regarding socialization and personality development.
2. To become aware of the effects of social isolation on humans and other primates.
3. To become aware of the key components of Sigmund Freud's model of personality.
4. To be able to identify and describe the four stages of Jean Piaget's cognitive development theory.

5.	To be able to identify and describe the stages of moral development as identified by Lawrence Kohlberg.
6.	To analyze Carol Gilligan's critique of Kohlberg's moral development model.
7.	To be able to identify and describe the stages of personality development as outlined by Erik Erikson.
8.	To consider the contributions of George Herbert Mead to the understanding of personality development.
9.	To be able to compare the spheres of socialization (family, school, etc.) in terms of their effects on an individual's socialization experiences.
10.	To develop a life-course perspective of the socialization experience.
11.	To begin to understand the cross-cultural and historical patterns of death and dying as part of the life course.
12.	To be able to discuss the sociological perspective on socialization as a constraint to freedom.

PART III: KEY CONCEPTS

adolescence
adulthood
ageism
anticipatory socialization
behaviorism
childhood
cognition
cohort
concrete operations stage
ego
eros
formal operations stage
game stage
generalized other
I
id
looking-glass self
hidden curriculum
hurried child syndrome
institutionalized
mass media
me
old age
peer group
personality
preoperational stage
resocialization
repression
self
sensorimotor stage

significant other
social behaviorism
socialization
sublimation
superego
taking the role of the other
thanatos
total institution

PART IV: IMPORTANT RESEARCHERS

Kingsley Davis

John Watson

Harry and Margaret Harlow

Sigmund Freud

Jean Piaget

Lawrence Kohlberg

Carol Gilligan

Charles Horton Cooley

George Herbert Mead

Elisabeth Kubler-Ross

Erik H. Erikson

Charles Darwin

PART V: STUDY QUESTIONS

True-False

1.	T	F	As defined by our author, the concept of *personality* does not concern actual behavior.
2.	T	F	John Watson was a nineteenth-century psychologist who argued that human behavior was largely determined by *heredity*.
3.	T	F	The Harlows' research on rhesus monkeys concerning *social isolation* illustrates that while short-term isolation can be overcome, long-term isolation appears to cause irreversible emotional and behavioral damage to monkeys.
4.	T	F	The cases of *Isabelle, Anna,* and *Genie* support the arguments made by naturalists that certain personality characteristics are determined by heredity.
5.	T	F	Sigmund Freud envisioned *biological factors* as having little or no influence on personality development.
6.	T	F	The *id* in Freud's pyschoanalytic theory represents the human being's basic needs which are unconscious and demand immediate satisfaction.
7.	T	F	According to Jean Piaget, language and other symbols are first used in the *preoperational stage.*
8.	T	F	According to Lawrence Kohlberg, during the *preconventional stage* of moral development, a person defines "rightness" in terms of "what feels good to me."
9.	T	F	Carol Gilligan's research focuses on how *gender* affects *moral reasoning.*
10.	T	F	George Herbert Mead argued that *biological factors* played *little or no* role in the development of the self.
11.	T	F	George Herbert Mead refers to *taking the role of the other* as the interplay between the *I* and *me.*
12.	T	F	George Herbert Mead's concept of the *generalized other* refers to widespread cultural norms and values shared by us and others that we use as a reference point to evaluate ourselves.
13.	T	F	According to George Herbert Mead, the objective side of the self is known as the *me.*
14.	T	F	According to Erik H. Erikson's theory personality formation is a lifelong process.
15.	T	F	The concept *hidden curriculum* relates to the important cultural values being transmitted to children in school.
16.	T	F	A *peer group* is a social group whose members have interests, social positions, and age in common.
17.	T	F	Children in the United States spend as much time watching television as they do going to school.
18.	T	F	The study of childhood is known as *gerontology.*
19.	T	F	The percentage of our society's population over the age of sixty-five has been *declining* over the last several decades.
20.	T	F	A *cohort* is a setting in which people are isolated from the rest of society and manipulated by an administrative staff.

Multiple Choice

1. The story of *Anna* illustrates the significance of _____ in personality development.

    (a) heredity
    (b) social interaction
    (c) physical conditions
    (d) ecology

2. The lifelong social experience by which individuals develop their human potential and learn culture is called:

    (a) socialization.
    (b) personality.
    (c) adjustment.
    (d) adaptation.
    (e) behaviorism.

3. A person's fairly constant patterns of acting, thinking, and feeling is called:

    (a) socialization.
    (b) personality.
    (c) behaviorism.
    (d) reasoning.

4. The perspective developed by the psychologist John Watson, claiming that human behavior is not instinctive, but learned within a social environment is termed:

    (a) naturalism.
    (b) psychology.
    (c) sociology.
    (d) evolution.
    (e) behaviorism.

5. The major tenet of *behaviorism* is that:

    (a) behavior patterns are instinctive, not learned.
    (b) behavior patterns are learned, not instinctive.
    (c) humans are culturally similar around the world.
    (d) feelings and thoughts connected to behaviors are more important than the behaviors themselves..

6. What did the experiments on social isolation among rhesus monkeys show?

    (a) Artificial monkeys provided sufficient contact for young monkeys to develop normally.
    (b) The behavior of rhesus monkey infants is totally dissimilar to human infants.
    (c) Deprivation of social experience, rather than the absence of a specific parent, has devastating effects.
    (d) Biological forces in rhesus monkeys cushions them from the negative effects of social isolation.

7. Which of the following is representative of *Sigmund Freud's* analysis of personality?

    (a) Biological forces play only a small role in personality development.
    (b) The term instinct is understood as very general human needs in the form of urges and drives.
    (c) The most significant period for personality development is adolescence.
    (d) Personality is best studied as a process of externalizing social forces.

8. *Sigmund Freud's* model of personality does *not* include which of the following elements?

    (a) superego
    (b) id
    (c) self
    (d) ego

9. Culture existing within the individual *Sigmund Freud* called:

    (a) thanatos.
    (b) eros.
    (c) the ego.
    (d) the id.
    (e) the superego.

10. In Sigmund Freud's model of personality, what balances the innate pleasure-seeking drive with the demands of society?

    (a) id
    (b) ego
    (c) superego
    (d) thanatos

11. According to *Jean Piaget*, which of the following best describes the *preoperational stage* of cognitive development?

   (a)   the level of human development in which the world is experienced only through sensory contact
   (b)   the level of human development characterized by the use of logic to understand objects and events
   (c)   the level of human development in which language and other symbols are first used
   (d)   the level of human development characterized by highly abstract thought

12. Jean Piaget's focus was on:

   (a)   how children develop fine motor skills.
   (b)   how children are stimulated by their environment.
   (c)   cognition--how people think and understand.
   (d)   the role of heredity in determining human behavior.

13. According to *Jean Piaget's* cognitive development theory, the _____ stage refers to a level of development at which individuals first perceive causal connections in their surroundings.

   (a)   preoperational
   (b)   conventional
   (c)   play
   (d)   concrete operations

14. In *Lawrence Kohlberg's* moral development theory the _____ level refers to the period during which people shed some of their selfishness as they learn to define right and wrong in terms of what pleases parents and what fits with cultural norms.

   (a)   conventional
   (b)   preconventional
   (c)   postconventional
   (d)   operational
   (e)   imitative

15. According to research by *Carol Gilligan*, males use a _____ perspective concerning moral reasoning.

   (a)   justice
   (b)   independent
   (c)   visual
   (d)   mechanical

16. *George Herbert Mead's* perspective has often been described as:

    (a)   psychological pragmatism.
    (b)   behaviorism.
    (c)   social behaviorism.
    (d)   psychoanalysis.
    (e)   naturalism.

17. The concept of the *looking-glass self* refers to:

    (a)   Freud's argument that through psychoanalysis a person can uncover the unconscious.
    (b)   Piaget's view that through biological maturation and social experience individuals become able to logically hypothesize about thoughts without relying on concrete reality.
    (c)   Watson's behaviorist notion that one can see through to a person's mind only by observing the person's behavior.
    (d)   Cooley's idea that the self-image we have is based on how we suppose others perceive us.

18. George Herbert Mead used the term _____ to describe the widespread cultural norms and values shared by us and others that we use as a point of reference in evaluating ourselves.

    (a)   looking-glass self
    (b)   socialization
    (c)   significant other
    (d)   generalized other

19. According to *George Herbert Mead,* all symbolic interaction involves seeing ourselves as others see us—a process he called _____.

    (a)   repression
    (b)   taking the role of the other
    (c)   imitation
    (d)   cognition
    (e)   sublimation

20. The first stage in *George Herbert Mead's* developmental theory of the social self is:

    (a)   play.
    (b)   imitation.
    (c)   game
    (d)   play.

21. *Erik H. Erikson's* view on socialization is best defined by which of the following statements?

    (a)   Human personality is primarily formed in the first year of life.
    (b)   We use others as a reference point for evaluating ourselves as we grow.
    (c)   The superego and the id are in continual conflict as we grow and change.
    (d)   Personality changes throughout the life cycle as we face challenges at different stages of life.

22. The process of social learning directed toward assuming a desired status and role in the future is called:

    (a)   resocialization.
    (b)   socialization.
    (c)   looking-glass self.
    (d)   anticipatory socialization.

23. The _____ are impersonal communications directed at a vast audience.

    (a)   mass media
    (b)   total institution
    (c)   hidden curriculum
    (d)   generalized other

24. Which of the following is *not* one of the three distinctive characteristics of a *total institution*?

    (a)   staff members supervise all spheres of daily life
    (b)   staff members encourage the maintenance of individuality, and encourage creativity
    (c)   food, sleeping quarters and activities are standardized
    (d)   formal rules dictate how virtually every moment is spent

25. _____ refers to a process of radically altering the personality through deliberate manipulation of the environment.

    (a)   Anticipatory socialization
    (b)   Resocialization
    (c)   Primary socialization
    (d)   Degradation

Matching

1. ____ A person's fairly consistent patterns of acting, thinking, and feeling.
2. ____ The operation of culture within the individual.
3. ____ Deliberate socialization intended to radically alter the individual's personality.
4. ____ A category of people with a common characteristic, usually their age.
5. ____ The self-image we have based on how we suppose others perceive us.
6. ____ A group whose members have interests, social position, and age in common.
7. ____ A theory developed by John Watson that holds that behavior patterns are not instinctive but learned.

8. ____ A setting in which individuals are isolated from the rest of society and manipulated by an administrative staff.
9. ____ Impersonal communications directed to a vast audience.
10. ____ In Piaget's theory, the level of development at which individuals perceive causal connections in their surroundings.
11. ____ According to George Herbert Mead, the subjective side of the self.
12. ____ According to Elisabeth Kubler-Ross, a person's first reaction to the prospect of dying.

a.	looking-glass self	f	superego	k.	me
b.	behaviorism	g.	cohort	l.	I
c.	mass media	h.	peer group	m.	negotiation
d.	concrete operational stage	i.	Personality	n.	denial
e.	resocialization	j.	total institution		

Fill-In

1. A _____ is defined as a person's fairly consistent pattern of acting, thinking, and feeling.

2. The approach called _____ developed by *John Watson* in the early twentieth century provided a perspective that stressed learning rather than instincts as the key to personality development.

3. According to *Sigmund Freud*, the _____ represents a person's conscious efforts to balance the innate pleasure-seeking drives of the human organism and the demands of society.

4. *Sigmund Freud* argued that culture , in the form of the superego serves to _____, whereas he called the process of transforming fundamentally selfish drives into more socially acceptable objectives _____.

5. *Jean Piaget's* work centered on human _____.

6. *Lawrence Kohlberg* identifies three stages in moral development, these include the _____, the _____, and the _____.

7. *Carol Gilligan* suggests that boys tend to use a *justice perspective* in moral reasoning, relying on formal rules in reaching a judgement about right and wrong. On the other hand, says Gilligan, girls tend to use a _____ and _____ *perspective* in moral reasoning, which leads them to judge a situation with an eye toward personal relationships.

8. *George Herbert Mead* explained that infants with limited social experience respond to others only in terms of _____.

9. According to the developmental theory of *Erik H. Erikson*, the third stage (pre-school) involves the challenge of initiative versus _____.

10. The process of social learning directed toward gaining a desired position is called _____ *socialization*.

11. Impersonal communications directed to a vast audience refers to the _____.

12. A _____ is a form of social organization in which the elderly have the most wealth, power, and privileges.

13. *Elisabeth Kubler-Ross* described death as an orderly transition involving five stages, including _____, _____, _____, _____, and _____.

14. Prisons and mental hospitals are examples of _____.

Definition and Short-Answer

1. How did the work of *Charles Darwin* influence the understanding of personality development in the last nineteenth century?
2. What was *John Watson's* view concerning personality development?
3. Review the research by *Harry* and *Margaret Harlow* on social isolation. What were the important discoveries they made?
4. Discuss the cases of *childhood isolation* presented in the text. What are the important conclusions being drawn from these cases?
5. Identify and define the parts of personality as seen by *Sigmund Freud*.
6. What are the four stages of cognitive development according to *Jean Piaget*? Briefly describe the qualities of each stage. What is one major criticism of his theory?
7. What are the stages of personality development according to Erik Erikson? In what two important ways does his theory differ from Sigmund Freud's?
8. Define the concept *looking-glass self*. Provide an illustration of this concept from your own personal experience.
9. Define and differentiate between the terms *generalized other* and *significant other*. Further, what are the four basic arguments being made by *George Herbert Mead* concerning personality development?
10. According to the text, what are the four important *agents of socialization*? Provide an illustration of how each is involved in the socialization process.
11. What are the stages of *adulthood* and the qualities of each?
12. What is a *total institution*? What are the typical experiences of a person who is living within a total institution? How do these experiences affect personality development?
13. Based on the sociological research cited in this chapter, to what extent can it be argued that humans are like "puppets" in society?
14. What conclusions are being made by the author concerning the *life course*?

PART VI: ANSWERS TO STUDY QUESTIONS

True-False

1.	F	(p. 61)		11.	T	(p. 68)
2.	F	(p. 62)		12.	T	(p. 68)
3.	T	(p. 63)		13.	T	(p. 68)
4.	F	(p. 63)		14.	T	(p. 69)
5.	F	(p. 64)		15.	T	(p. 70)
6.	T	(p. 64)		16.	T	(p. 71)
7.	T	(p. 65)		17.	T	(p. 72)
8.	T	(p. 66)		18.	F	(p. 76)
9.	T	(p. 67)		19.	F	(p. 77)
10.	T	(p. 67)		20.	F	(p. 79)

Multiple Choice

1.	b	(p. 61)	14.	a	(p. 66)
2.	a	(p. 61)	15.	a	(p. 67)
3.	b	(p. 61)	16.	c	(p. 67)
4.	e	(p. 62)	17.	d	(p. 68)
5.	b	(p. 62)	18.	d	(p. 68)
6.	c	(p. 63)	19.	b	(p. 68)
7.	b	(p. 64)	20.	b	(p. 68)
8.	c	(p. 64)	21.	d	(p. 69)
9.	e	(p. 64)	22.	d	(p. 71)
10.	b	(p. 64)	23.	a	(p. 71)
11.	c	(p. 65)	24.	b	(p. 80)
12.	c	(p. 65)	25.	b	(p. 80)
13.	d	(p. 65)			

Matching

1.	i	(p. 61)	7.	b	(p. 62)
2.	f	(p. 64)	8.	e	(p. 80)
3.	e	(p. 80)	9.	c	(p. 71)
4.	g	(p. 79)	10.	d	(p. 75)
5.	a	(p. 68)	11.	l	(p. 68)
6.	h	(p. 71)	12.	n	(p. 78)

Fill-In

1. personality (p. 61)
2. behaviorism (p. 62)
3. ego (p. 64)
4. repress, sublimation (p. 64)
5. cognition (p. 65)
6. preconventional, conventional, postconventional (p. 66)
7. care, responsibility (p. 67)
8. imitation (p. 68)
9. guilt (p. 69)
10. anticipatory (p. 68)
11 mass media (p. 71)
12. gerontocracy (p.77)
13. denial, negotiation, anger, resignation, acceptance (pp. 78-79)
14. Total institution (p. 80)

PART VII: IN FOCUS—MAJOR ISSUES

- Review the major points concerning the impact of *social isolation* on human development. Make specific reference to the Harlow's research with monkeys and the research on isolated children.

- Identify and define the elements of personality according to *Sigmund Freud.*

- Describe each of the following stages in *Jean Piaget's* cognitive development model.

  Sensorimotor:

  Preoperational:

  Concrete Operational:

  Formal Operational:

- Describe each of the three levels of moral development according to *Lawrence Kohlberg.*

  Preconventional:

  Conventional:

  Postconventional:

- Identify and describe the four major ideas *George Herbert Mead* connected to the concept of *self.*

- Describe each of the following stages in the developmental theory of *George Herbert Mead.*

  Imitation:

  Play:

  Game:

  Generalized Other:

- Identify the eight stages (and corresponding challenges) found in the developmental theory of *Erik H. Erikson.*

- Review one major point made in the text concerning each of the following *agents of socialization.*

  The Family: The Peer Group:

  The School: The Mass Media:

PART VIII: ANALYSIS AND COMMENT

Social Diversity

"How Do the Media Portray Minorities?"

Key Points: Questions:

Controversy and Debate

"Are We Free Within Society?"

Key Points: Questions:

Window on the World--Global Map 5-1

"Child Labor in Global Perspective"

Key Points: Questions:

Seeing Ourselves--National Map 5-1

"Television Viewing and Newspaper Reading across the United States"

Key Points: Questions:

4 Social Interaction In Everyday Life

PART I: CHAPTER OUTLINE

PART II: LEARNING OBJECTIVES

1.   To be able to identify the characteristics of social structure.
2.   To be able to discuss the relationship between social structure and individuality.
3.   To be able to distinguish between the different types of statuses and roles.
4.   To be able to describe and illustrate the social construction of reality.

5. To begin to see how the technological capacity of a society influences the social construction of reality.
6. To be able to describe and illustrate the approach known as ethnomethodology.
7. To see the importance of performance, nonverbal communication, idealization, and embarrassment to the "presentation of the self."
8. To be able to describe and illustrate dramaturgical analysis.
9. To be able to use gender and humor as illustrations of how people construct meaning in everyday life.

PART III: KEY CONCEPTS

achieved status
ascribed status
dramaturgical analysis
ethnomethodology
humor
idealization
master status
nonverbal communication
performance
personal space
presentation of self
role
role conflict
role exit
role expectations
role performance
role set
role strain
social interaction
status
status set
social construction of reality
Thomas theorem

PART IV: IMPORTANT RESEARCHERS

Robert Merton   Harold Garfinkel

Erving Goffman   Paul Ekman

PART V: STUDY QUESTIONS

True-False

1.	T	F	A *status* refers to a pattern of expected behavior for individual members of society.
2.	T	F	Status is not related to social identity.
3.	T	F	A *status set* refers to all statuses a person holds during his or her lifetime.
4.	T	F	Both *statuses* and *roles* vary by culture.
5.	T	F	*Role strain* refers to the incompatibility among roles corresponding to a single status.
6.	T	F	The phrase *the social construction of reality* relates to the sociologist's view that statuses and roles structure our lives along narrowly delineated paths.
7.	T	F	The *Thomas theorem* states that statuses expand to accommodate the number of roles occupied by the individual holding those statuses.
8.	T	F	For the *ethnomethodologist*, a deliberate lack of social cooperation may lead the researcher to see more clearly the unspoken rules of everyday life.
9.	T	F	According to *Erving Goffman, performances* are very rigidly scripted, leaving virtually no room for individual adaptation.
10.	T	F	Cross-cultural research suggests virtually all *nonverbal communication* is universally understood.
11.	T	F	According to research on gender and personal performances, men use significantly more space than women.
12.	T	F	According to *Erving Goffman's* research, *tact* is relatively uncommon in our society.
13.	T	F	According to dramaturgical analysis, *embarrassment* causes discomfort for both the presenter and the audience.
14.	T	F	A foundation of *humor* lies in the contrast between two incongruous realities--the *conventional* and *unconventional*.
15.	T	F	One trait of humorous material which appears to be universal is controversy.

Multiple-Choice

1. What is the term for a recognized social position that an individual occupies?

    (a) prestige
    (b) status
    (c) social power
    (d) role
    (e) dramaturgy

2. A friend of yours is a daughter, mother, sister, friend, employee, and golfer. All these taken together are your friend's:

    (a) Status.
    (b) role configuration.
    (c) role complex.
    (d) status set.

3.   Which of the following is *not* a structural component of social interaction?

   (a)   master status
   (b)   role
   (c)   value
   (d)   role set
   (e)   ascribed status

4.   *Ralph Linton* described _____ as the dynamic expression of a status.

   (a)   master status
   (b)   role
   (c)   performance
   (d)   dramaturgy
   (e)   nonverbal communication

5.   What is the term for a status that has exceptional importance for social identity, often shaping a person's entire life?

   (a)   role
   (b)   ascribed status
   (c)   achieved status
   (d)   master status
   (e)   role set

6.   What is the term for patterns of expected behavior attached to a particular status?

   (a)   role
   (b)   master status
   (c)   achieved status
   (d)   ascribed status

7.   The incompatibility among the roles corresponding to two or more statuses refers to:

   (a)   role conflict.
   (b)   role strain.
   (c)   status overload.
   (d)   status inconsistency.
   (e)   role set.

8.   Methods of reducing *role strain* include which of the following?

(a)   discarding one or more roles
(b)   compartmentalizing roles
(c)   emphasizing some roles more than others
(d)   all of the above
(e)   none of the above

9.   The process by which individuals creatively shape reality through social interaction is called:

(a)   reality construction.
(b)   the social construction of reality.
(c)   creative reality.
(d)   interactive reality.

10.   The *Thomas theorem* states:

(a)   roles are only as important as the statuses to which they are attached.
(b)   statuses are only as important as the roles on which they are dependent.
(c)   the basis of humanity is built upon the dual existence of creativity and conformity.
(d)   common sense is only as good as the social structure within which it is embedded.
(e)   situations defined as real become real in their consequences.

11.   What is the term for the study of the way people make sense of their everyday lives?

(a)   naturalism
(b)   phenomenology
(c)   ethnomethodology
(d)   social psychology

12.   The approach used by *ethnomethodologists* to study everyday interaction involves:

(a)   conducting surveys.
(b)   unobtrusive observation.
(c)   secondary analysis.
(d)   breaking rules.
(e)   laboratory experiment.

13.   The investigation of social interaction in terms of *theatrical performance* is referred to as:

(a)   ethnomethodology.
(b)   dramaturgical analysis.
(c)   theatrical analysis.
(d)   phenomenology.

14. The process of the *presentation of the self* is also known as:

    (a) ethnomethodology.
    (b) achieved status.
    (c) idealization.
    (d) ascribed status.
    (e) impression management.

15. *Mr. Preedy*, the fictional character introduced in the text, provides an example of:

    (a) role conflict.
    (b) role strain.
    (c) nonverbal communication.
    (d) status inconsistency.

16. What is *demeanor*?

    (a) general conduct and deportment
    (b) a non-felony crime
    (c) a form of mental illness
    (d) gender-specific activity

17. Helping a person to "save face," or avoid embarrassment, is called:

    (a) diplomacy.
    (b) generosity.
    (c) altruism.
    (d) tact.

18. Which of the following is *not* an example provided in the text to illustrate how *language* functions to define the sexes?

    (a) the attention function
    (b) the power function
    (c) the value function
    (d) the affective function

19. *Humor* is generated by:

    (a) mixing together opposing tendencies.
    (b) miscommunication.
    (c) combining embarrassment and tact.
    (d) confusing intent and meaning.

20.   Which of the following is *not* a *function of humor*?

    (a)   Humor can be a stimulant to social change.
    (b)   Humor limits racism and sexism.
    (c)   Humor can be a safety valve.
    (d)   Humor can be used as a form of tact.

Matching

1.   _____   Expected behavior of someone who holds a particular status.
2.   _____   Incompatibility among roles corresponding to two or more statuses.
3.   _____   A social position a person receives at birth or assumes involuntarily later in life.
4.   _____   The process by which people act and react in relation to others.
5.   _____   The study of the way people make sense of their everyday lives.
6.   _____   The investigation of social interaction in terms of theatrical performance.
7.   _____   General conduct or deportment.
8.   _____   Situations defined as real become real in their consequences.
9.   _____   A recognized social position that an individual occupies.
10.   _____   Incompatibility among roles corresponding to a single status.

    a.   ascribed status   f.   role
    b.   ethnomethodology   g.   demeanor
    c.   Thomas theorem   h.   status
    d.   role strain   i.   dramaturgical analysis
    e.   social interaction   j.   role conflict

Fill-In

1.   _____ _____ refers to the process by which people act and react in relation to others.
2.   _____ refers to a recognized social position that an individual occupies in society, while _____ refers to patterns of expected behaviors attached to a particular status.
3.   An _____ *status* refers to a social position that a person receives at birth or assumes involuntarily later in life.
4.   _____ refers to the incompatibility among the roles corresponding to two or more statuses.
5.   The _____ _____ states that situations defined as real are real in their consequences.
6.   The study of everyday, common-sense understandings that people within a culture have of the world around them is known as _____.
7.   _____ *analysis* is the investigation of social interaction in terms of theatrical performance.
8.   _____ refers to ways in which individuals, in various settings, attempt to create specific impressions in the minds of others.

9. Props in a doctor's office, like books and framed diplomas, are examples of the _____ *region* of the setting.
10. According to Paul Ekman's cross-cultural studies, there are *six basic emotions* that are universally shared and expressed in similar ways. These include: _____, _____, _____ _____, _____, and _____.
11. According to *Erving Goffman*, _____ refers to general conduct or deportment.
12. When people try to convince others that what they are doing reflects ideal cultural standards rather than less virtuous motives, *Erving Goffman* said they are involved in _____.
13. Language defines men and women differently in at least three ways--in terms of _____, _____, and _____.
14. According to *Deborah Tannen*, women and men us language differently. The problem couples face in communicating is that what one partner _____ by a comment is not always what the other _____.
15. *Humor* stems from the contrast between two incongruous realities, the _____ and the _____.

Definition and Short-Answer

1. Review the story of the physician's office and *performances* in the text. Using this account as an example, select a social situation you have been involved in and do a dramaturgical analysis to describe its context.
2. Provide an illustration of *nonverbal communication* using the story of *Mr. Preedy* as a model.
3. What are some different types of information provided by a *performer* in terms of nonverbal communication which can be used to determine whether or not a person is telling the truth? Provide an illustration.
4. Refer to *Figure 4-1* (p. 88) and using it as a model, diagram your own status and role sets. Identify points of *role conflict* and *role strain*.
5. What are three ways in which language functions to define the sexes differently? Provide an illustration for each.
6. What is *ethnomethodology*?
7. Define the concept *idealization*. Provide an illustration using the doctor's office account as a model.
8. Provide an illustration of the *Thomas theorem* from experiences you have had either at home or in school.
9. What are the basic characteristics of *humor*? Write out a joke and analyze how it manifests the characteristics discussed in the text.

PART VI: ANSWERS TO STUDY QUESTIONS

True-False

1.	F	(p. 86)		9.	F	(p. 93)
2.	F	(p. 86)		10.	T	(p. 94)
3.	F	(p. 86)		11.	T	(p. 96)
4.	T	(p. 87)		12.	F	(p. 98)
5.	T	(p. 88)		13.	T	(p. 98)

6.	F	(p. 88)		14.	T	(p. 101)
7.	F	(p. 90)		15.	T	(p. 102)
8.	T	(p. 91)				

Multiple Choice

1.	b	(p. 86)		11.	c	(p. 91)
2.	d	(p. 86)		12.	d	(p. 91)
3.	c	(pp. 86-87)		13.	b	(p. 92)
4.	b	(p. 87)		14.	e	(p. 93)
5.	d	(p. 87)		15.	c	(p. 94)
6.	a	(p. 87)		16.	a	(p. 96)
7.	a	(p. 88)		17.	d	(p. 98)
8.	d	(p. 88)		18.	d	(p. 99)
9.	b	(p. 88)		19.	a	(p. 102)
10.	e	(p. 90)		20.	b	(p. 103)

Matching

1.	f	(p. 87)		6.	i	(p. 92)
2.	j	(p. 88)		7.	g	(p. 96)
3.	a	(p. 86)		8.	c	(p. 90)
4.	e	(p. 85)		9.	h	(p. 86)
5.	b	(p. 91)		10.	d	(p. 88)

Fill-In

1.	social interaction (p. 85)		9.	back (p. 93)
2.	status, role (pp. 86-87)		10.	anger, fear, happiness, disgust, surprise, sadness (p. 94)
3.	ascribed (p. 86)		11.	demeanor (p. 96)
4.	role conflict (p. 88)		12.	idealization (p. 97)
5.	Thomas theorem (p. 90)		13.	control, value, attention (p. 99)
6.	ethnomethodology (p. 91)		14.	intends, hears (p. 100)
7.	dramaturgical (p. 92)		15.	conventional, unconventional (p. 101)
8.	presentation of self (p. 93)			

PART VII: IN FOCUS—MAJOR ISSUES

• Define and illustrate the following components of *social structure*.

Status: Achieved Status: Ascribed Status:

Master Status: Status Set:

Role: Role Set:

Role Strain: Role Conflict:

Role Exit:

- Define and illustrate the following as each relates to the *social construction of reality*.

The Thomas theorem:

Street Smarts:

Ethnomethodology:

- Discuss *dramaturgical analysis* by illustrating the following concepts—*performances, nonverbal communication, gender and performance, idealization, embarrassment* and *tact*.

- Illustrate each of the following ways in which *language defines men and women*.

    Language and Power:

    Language and Value:

    Language and Attention:

- Using a joke or jokes to illustrate, provide evidence for the following:

    The *functions of humor:*

    The *dynamics of humor:*

    The *topics of humor:*

PART VIII: ANALYSIS AND COMMENT

Social Diversity

"Gender and Language: You Just Don't Understand!"

Key Points: Questions:

Critical Thinking

"The "Spin" Game: Choosing Our Words Carefully"

Key Points: Questions:

Sociology of Everyday Life

"Double Take: Real Headlines That Make People Laugh"

Key Points: Questions:

Global Sociology

"Emotions in Global Perspective: Feelings the Same Everywhere?"

Key Points: Questions:

Seeing Ourselves--National Map 4-1

"Baseball Fans Across the United States"

Key Points: Questions

Window on the World--Global Map 4-1

"Housework in Global Perspective"

Key Points: Questions:

5 | Groups and Organizations

PART I: CHAPTER OUTLINE

PART II: LEARNING OBJECTIVES

1. To be able to identify the differences between primary groups, secondary groups, aggregates, and categories.

2. To be able to identify the various types of leaders associated with social groups.
3. To be able to compare and contrast the research of several different social scientists on group conformity.
4. To be able to recognize the importance of reference groups to group dynamics.
5. To be able to distinguish between ingroups and outgroups.
6. To understand the relevance of group size to the dynamics of social groups.
7. To be able to identify the types of formal organizations.
8. To be able to identify and describe the basic characteristics of bureaucracy.
9. To become aware of both the limitations and informal side of bureaucracy.
10. To be able to consider ways of humanizing bureaucracy.
11. To consider the issue of the McDonaldization of society.
12. To analyze formal organizations from a cross-cultural perspective.

PART III: KEY CONCEPTS

aggregates
authoritarian leadership
bureaucracy
bureaucratic ritualism
category
coercive organization
crowd
democratic leadership
dyad
expressive leadership
formal organizations
groupthink
humanizing organizations
ingroup
instrumental leadership
laissez-faire leadership
McDonaldization
network
normative organization
oligarchy
organizational environment
outgroup
Parkinson's law
Peter principle
primary group
rationality
rationalization
reference group
secondary group

social group
tradition
triad
utilitarian organization

PART IV: IMPORTANT RESEARCHERS

Max Weber

George Simmel

Charles Horton Cooley

Amitai Etzioni

Stanley Milgram

Solomon Asch

Irving Janis

Samuel Stouffer

Rosabeth Moss Kanter

Robert Michels

William Ouchi

Deborah Tannen

Sally Helgesen

George Ritzer

PART V: STUDY QUESTIONS

True-False

1. T F While members of *categories* could potentially become transformed into a social group, by definition members of *crowds* cannot be transformed into social groups.
2. T F *Expressive leadership* emphasizes the completion of tasks.
3. T F *Stanley Milgram's* research on group conformity patterns illustrated that most individuals are skeptical about the legitimacy of authority for people in positions of power.
4. T F *Samuel Stouffer's* research on soldiers' attitudes toward their own promotions during World War II demonstrates the significance of reference groups in making judgments about ourselves.
5. T F According to research by *Georg Simmel*, large groups tend to be more stable than small groups, such as dyads.
6. T F *Networks* tend to be more enduring and provide a greater sense of identity than most other types of social groups.
7. T F *Normative organizations* are defined as those which impose restrictions on people who have been labeled as deviant.
8. T F According to *Max Weber*, diffusion of responsibility is a major element of bureaucratic organizations.
9. T F *Parkinson's Law* and the *Peter Principle* relate to processes of bureaucratic waste and incompetency.
10. T F Research on *self-managed work groups* demonstrates that those members of a bureaucracy who have restricted opportunities often are the people who demonstrate the most creativity and have the highest aspirations for achievement.
11. T F A basic organizational principle involved in the *McDonaldization of society* is efficiency.
12. T F Population patterns are part of the *organizational environment.*
13. T F *Irrational rationality* refers to the negative impact of polcies and programs to humanize formal organizations.
14. T F *Japanese* organizations include the characteristics of broad-based training, collective decision making, and holistic involvement.

Multiple Choice

1. What is the sociological term for all people with a *common status*, such as "college student?"

    (a) a crowd
    (b) a group
    (c) a category
    (d) a population
    (e) a social organization

2. A temporary cluster of individuals who may or may not interact is referred to as a:

   (a) population.
   (b) group.
   (c) category.
   (d) crowd.
   (e) social organization.

3. A social group characterized by long-term personal relationships usually involving many activities is a _____.

   (a) primary group
   (b) secondary group
   (c) category
   (d) aggregate
   (c) normative organization

4. Which of the following is *not* true of *primary groups*?

   (a) they provide security for their members
   (b) they are focused around specific activities
   (c) they are valued in and of themselves
   (d) they are viewed as ends in themselves

5. Which of the following theorists differentiated between *primary* and *secondary* groups?

   (a) Max Weber
   (b) Amitai Etzioni
   (c) Emile Durkheim
   (d) Charles Horton Cooley
   (e) George Herbert Mead

6. Which of the following is *not* a characteristic of a *secondary group*.

   (a) large size
   (b) weak emotional ties
   (c) personal orientation
   (d) variable, often short duration

7.   What is the term for a *group leadership* that emphasizes the completion of tasks?

(a)   task group leadership
(b)   secondary group leadership
(c)   expressive leadership
(d)   instrumental leadership
(e)   laissez-faire leadership

8.   Which of the following is *not* identified in the text as a *leadership style*?

(a)   laissez-faire
(b)   democratic
(c)   authoritarian
(d)   utilitarian

9.   Which *style of leadership* is least effective in promoting group goals?

(a)   instrumental
(b)   laissez-faire
(c)   authoritarian
(d)   democratic

10.   What *style of leader* tends to downplay their position and power, allowing the group to function more or less on its own?

(a)   authoritarian
(b)   democratic
(c)   laissez-faire
(d)   bureaucratic
(e)   instrumental

11.   Which researcher concluded that people are not likely to question authority figures even common sense dictates that they should?

(a)   Solomon Asch
(b)   Irving Janis
(c)   Stanley Milgram
(d)   Charles Horton Cooley

12. The Kennedy administration's decision to invade Cuba is used as an example of:

(a) ingroups and outgroups.
(b) reference groups.
(c) bureaucracy.
(d) oligarchy.
(e) groupthink.

13. What is the sociological term for a limited understanding of some issue due to group conformity?

(a) conformist cognizance
(b) groupthink
(c) doublethink
(d) red tape
(e) instrumentalism

14. The term for a social group that serves as a point of reference in making evaluations or decisions is:

(a) a control group
(b) a reference group
(c) an externalized group
(d) an internalized group

15. A social group commanding a member's esteem and loyalty is a(n):

(a) ingroup
(b) outgroup
(c) reference group
(d) subculture
(e) residual group

16. Large secondary groups that are organized to achieve their goals efficiently are referred to as:

(a) social organizations
(b) bureaucracies
(c) formal organizations
(d) businesses
(e) aggregates

17. *Amtitai Etzioni* constructed a typology of *formal organizations*. Organizations such as the PTA, the Red Cross, and United Way illustrate the type of organization he called:

   (a)   utilitarian.
   (b)   coercive.
   (c)   normative.
   (d)   utilitarian.

18. What types of *formal organizations* bestow material benefits on their members?

   (a)   normative organizations
   (b)   coercive organizations
   (c)   social organizations
   (d)   utilitarian organizations
   (e)   hierarchial organizations

19. Which of the following is *not* a type of formal organization as identified by *Amitai Etzioni*?

   (a)   coercive
   (b)   normative
   (c)   hierarchial
   (d)   utilitarian

20. What term refers to an *organizational model* rationally designed to perform complex tasks efficiently?

   (a)   bureaucracy
   (b)   complex organization
   (c)   humanized organization
   (d)   social organization
   (e)   formal organization

21. *Bureaucratic ritualism* is:

   (a)   the process of promoting people to their level of incompetence
   (b)   the tendency of bureaucratic organizations to persist over time
   (c)   the rule of the many by the few
   (d)   a preoccupation with rules and regulations to the point of thwarting an organizations goals

22. *Robert Michels* identified one of the limitations of bureaucracy which involves the tendency of bureaucracy to become dominated by *oligarchy* because:

   (a)   technical competence cannot be maintained
   (b)   bureaucrats abuse organizational power
   (c)   bureaucrats get caught up in rule-making
   (d)   specialization gives way to generalist orientations

23. _____ refers to the fact that bureaucrats are promoted to the level of their *incompetence*.

    (a)   Boyle's law.
    (b)   The Peter Principle.
    (c)   Parkinson's law.
    (d)   Durheimian analysis.
    (e)   Oligarchy.

24. According to *Rosabeth Moss Kanter's* research:

    (a)   proper application of technology in bureaucracy is critical for success
    (b)   oligarchy is effective in bureaucratic structures during times of rapid change
    (c)   race and gender issues must be addressed as they relate to organizational hierarchies
    (d)   humanizing bureaucracies would diminish productivity
    (e)   none of the above

25. Which of the following is *not* identified by *Sally Helgesen* as a gender-linked issue in organizations?

    (a)   attentiveness to interconnections
    (b)   flexibility
    (c)   worker productivity
    (d)   communication skills

26. Which of the following is/are included in the *organizational environment*?

    (a)   technology
    (b)   economic and political trends
    (c)   population patterns
    (d)   other organizations
    (e)   all of the above

27. According to *George Ritzer*, which of the following is/are characteristic of the *McDonaldization* of society?

    (a)   efficiency
    (b)   calculability
    (c)   predictability
    (d)   control through automation
    (e)   all of the above are

28. According to *William Ouchi* which of the following highlights the distinctions between formal organizations in Japan and the United States?

   (a) hiring and advancement, lifetime security, holistic involvement, nonspecialized training, and collective decision making
   (b) predictability, calculability, control through automation, and efficiency
   (c) oligarchy, ritualism, privacy, and alienation
   (d) competence, tasks, inertia, and networks

Matching

1. ___ The tendency of group members to conform by adopting a narrow view of some issue.
2. ___ A social group that serves as a point of reference in making evaluations or decisions.
3. ___ A small social group in which relationships are personal and enduring.
4. ___ Two or more people who identify and interact with one another.
5. ___ People who share a status in common.
6. ___ Group leaders who emphasize the completion of tasks.
7. ___ Large and impersonal groups based on a specific interest or activity.
8. ___ A social group with two members.
9. ___ Large, secondary groups that are organized to achieve their goals efficiently.
10. ___ An organizational model rationally designed to perform complex tasks efficiently.

   a. secondary
   b. formal organization
   c. groupthink
   d. instrumental leadership
   e. social group

   f. reference group
   g. dyad
   h. bureaucracy
   i. primary group
   j. category

Fill-In

1. A _____ _____ is defined as two or more people who identify and interact with one another.
2. Political organizations and college classes are examples of _____ *groups.*
3. While *primary* relationships have a _____ orientation, *secondary* relationships have a _____ orientation.
4. _____ *leadership* refers to group leadership that emphasizes the completion of tasks.
5. _____ *leaders* focus on instrumental concerns, make decisions on their own, and demand strict compliance from subordinates.
6. *Irving Janis* studies the process he called _____ that reduces a group's capacity for critical reflection.
7. A social group that consists of *two* members is known as a _____.

8. Peter Blau points out three ways in which the *social diversity* influences intergroup contact, including large groups turn _____, _____ groups turn outward, and physical boundaries foster _____ boundaries.

9. A _____ is a web of social ties that links people who identify and interact little with one another.

10. Amitai Etzioni has identified three *type of formal organizations*, distinguished by why people participate in them. Ones that pay their members are called _____ organizations. People become members of _____ organizations to pursue goals they consider morally worthwhile. Finally, _____ organizations are distinguished by involuntary membership.

11. A _____ is an organizational model rationally designed to perform complex tasks efficiently.

12. Preoccupation with rules and regulations to the point of thwarting an organization's goals is called *bureaucratic* _____.

13. *Bureaucratic* _____ is the term used to describe the tendency of bureaucratic organizations to perpetuate themselves.

14. *Deborah Tannen's* research on management styles suggests that women have a greater _____ *focus* and men have greater _____ focus.

15. Three paths are identified to a more *open* and *humane* organizational structure, including *social* _____, *sharing* _____, and _____ *opportunities for advancement.*

16. The *organizational environment* includes several dimensions, including _____, _____ and _____ *trends,* _____*patterns,* and other _____.

17. The four characteristics of the *McDonaldization of society* include _____, _____, _____ and _____, and _____ *through automation.*

18. The five basic principles of *Japanese organizations* are _____ and _____, *lifetime* _____, _____ *environment,* broad-based _____, and _____ *decision making.*

19. The success of Japanese organizations is due to their foundation of social solidarity and emphasis on _____ rather than individual achievement.

20. *National Map 5-2* focuses our attention on concern about _____ across the U.S.

Definition and Short-Answer

1. Differentiate between the qualities of *bureaucracies* and *small groups*. In what ways are they similar?
2. What are the three factors in decision-making processes in groups that lead to *groupthink*?
3. What are three major *limitations* of bureaucracy? Define and provide an illustration for each.
4. In what ways do bureaucratic organizations in *Japan* differ from those in the *U.S.*? What are the consequences of these differences? Relate this comparison to the issue of *humanizing* organizations.
5. Differentiate between the concepts of *aggregate* and *category*.
6. Identify the basic *types of leadership* in groups and provide examples of the relative advantages and disadvantage for each type.

7. What are the general characteristics of the *McDonaldization* of society? Provide an illustration of this phenomenon in our society based on your own experience.

8. What are the three paths to *humanizing organizations*? How does the research of Rosabeth Kanter relate to this issue?

9. What are Peter Blau's points concerning how the structure of social groups regulates intergroup association?

10. What are the three *types of organizations* identified by Amitai Etzioni? Describe and provide an illustration for each.

PART VI: ANSWERS TO STUDY QUESTIONS

True-False

1.	F	(p. 108)	8.	F	(p. 118)
2.	F	(p. 109)	9.	T	(p. 121)
3.	F	(pp. 110-111)	10.	F	(p. 123)
4.	T	(p. 112)	11.	T	(p. 124)
5.	T	(p. 113)	12.	T	(p. 124)
6.	F	(p. 114)	13.	F	(p. 125)
7.	F	(pp. 116-117)	14.	T	(p. 126)

Multiple Choice

1.	a	(p. 107)	15.	a	(p. 113)
2.	c	(p. 107)	16.	c	(p. 115)
3.	d	(p. 108)	17.	c	(pp. 116-117)
4.	b	(p. 108)	18.	d	(p. 117)
5.	d	(p. 108)	19.	c	(p. 116-117)
6.	c	(p. 108)	20.	a	(p. 117)
7.	d	(p. 109)	21.	d	(p. 120)
8.	d	(pp. 109-110)	22.	b	(pp. 120-121)
9.	c	(p. 110)	23.	c	(p. 121)
10.	c	(p. 110)	24.	d	(p. 122)
11.	c	(p. 110)	25.	c	(p. 122)
12.	e	(p. 111)	26.	e	(pp. 123-124)
13.	b	(p. 111)	27.	e	(pp. 124-125)
14.	b	(p. 112)	28.	a	(pp. 125-126)

Matching

1.	c	(p. 111)	6.	d	(p. 109)
2.	f	(p. 115)	7.	a	(p. 108)
3.	i	(p. 111)	8.	g	(p. 113)
4.	e	(p. 109)	9.	b	(p. 115)
5.	j	(p. 107)	10.	h	(p. 117)

1. social group (p. 107)
2. secondary (p. 108)
3. personal, goal (p. 108)
4. instrumental (p. 109)
5. authoritarian (p. 109)
6. groupthink (p. 111)
7. dyad (p. 113)
8. inward, heterogeneous, social (p. 114)
9. network (p. 114)
10. utilitarian, normative, coercive (pp. 116-117)
11. bureaucracy (p. 117)
12. ritualism (p. 120)
13. inertia (p. 120)
14. information, image (p. 122)
15. flexible, open, subordinate (p. 122)
16. technology, political, economic, population, organizations (pp. 123-124)
17. efficiency, calculability, uniformity, predictability, control (pp. 124-125)
18. hiring, advancement, security, holistic, training, collective (pp. 125-126)
19. groupism (p. 127)
20. privacy (p. 127)

PART VII: IN FOCUS—MAJOR ISSUES

- Identify the major characteristics of the following *types of group.*:

    primary group: secondary group:

- Differentiate between the following *types of leadership.*

    instrumental leadership: expressive leadership:

- Differentiate between the following *styles of leadership*:

    authoritarian leadership:

    democratic leadership:

    laissez-faire leadership:

- Define and illustrate the following *types of formal organizations*.

    normative:

    coercive:

    utilitarian:

- Identify and define the six *elements of the ideal bureaucratic organization*.

- Define and illustrate the following *problems of bureaucracy*.

    bureaucratic alienation: bureaucratic waste and incompetence:

    bureaucratic inertia: oligarchy:

- Identify and illustrate the four *basic principles of the "McDonaldization of society."*

- Identify five major distinctions between formal organizations in *Japan* and the *United States*.

PART VIII: ANALYSIS AND COMMENT

Exploring Cyber-Society

"The Internet: Welcome to Cyberspace"

Key Points: Questions:

Controversy and Debate

"Are Large Organizations a Threat to Personal Privacy?"

Key Points: Questions:

Seeing Ourselves--National Map 5-1

"The Quality of Relationships: Lawsuits across the United States"

Key Points: Questions:

Seeing Ourselves--National Map 5-2

"Concerns About Privacy Across the United States"

Key Points: Questions:

Window on the World--Global Map 5-1

"Cyberspace: A Global Network"

Key Points: Questions:

6 | Deviance

PART I: CHAPTER OUTLINE

I.   What is Deviance?
- A.   The Biological Context
- B.   Personality Factors
- C.   The Social Foundations of Deviance

II.   Structural-Functional Analysis
- A.   Durkheim's Basic Insight
- B.   Merton's Strain Theory
- C.   Deviant Subcultures

III.   Symbolic-Interaction Analysis
- A.   Labeling Theory
- B.   Primary and Secondary Deviance
- C.   Stigma
- D.   The Medicalization of Deviance
- E.   Sutherland's Differential Association Theory
- F.   Hirschi's Control Theory

IV.   Social Conflict Analysis
- A.   Deviance and Power
- B.   Deviance and Capitalism
- C.   White-Collar Crime

V.   Deviance and Social Diversity
- A.   Deviance and Gender
- B.   Hate Crimes

VI.   Crime
- A.   Types of Crime
- B.   Criminal Statistics
- C.   The "Street" Criminal: A Profile
- D.   Crime in Global Perspective

VII.   The Criminal Justice System
- A.   Police
- B.   Courts
- C.   Punishment

VIII.   Summary
  IX.   Key Concepts
   X.   Critical-Thinking Questions
  XI.   Learning Exercises

PART II: LEARNING OBJECTIVES

1.   To be able to explain how deviance is interpreted as a product of society.
2.   To be able to identify and evaluate the biological explanation of deviance.
3.   To be able to identify and evaluate the psychological explanation of deviance.
4.   To be able to identify and evaluate the sociological explanations of deviance.
5.   To be able to compare and contrast different theories representative of the three major sociological paradigms.
6.   To be able to evaluate empirical evidence used to support these different sociological theories of deviance.
7.   To be able to distinguish among the types of crime.
8.   To become more aware of the demographic patterns of crime in our society.
9.   To evaluate deviance in global context.
10.   To be able to identify and describe the elements of our criminal justice system.

PART III: KEY CONCEPTS

civil law
containment theory
conflict subculture
conformity
control theory
crime
crimes against property
crimes against the person
criminal justice system
criminal law
criminal recidivism
criminal subculture
deterrence
deviance
differential association
index crime
juvenile delinquency
labeling theory
medicalization of deviance

mesomorph
plea bargaining
primary deviance
rebellion
rehabilitation
retreatism
retreatist subculture
retribution
retrospective labeling
secondary deviance
social control
social protection
stigma
white-collar crime
victimless crime
victimization survey

PART IV: IMPORTANT RESEARCHERS

Caesare Lombroso   William Sheldon

Steven Spitzer   Richard Cloward and Lloyd Ohlin

Charles Goring   Albert Cohen and Walter Miller

Walter Reckless and Simon Dintz   Edwin Sutherland

Thomas Szaz   Emile Durkheim

Robert Merton   Travis Hirschi

Howard Becker   Erving Goffman

PART V: STUDY QUESTIONS

True-False

1.	T	F	Using the sociological perspective, *social control* is broadly understood, including the criminal justice system as well as the general socialization process.
2.	T	F	There is absolutely no relationship between *biology* and crime.
3.	T	F	*Containment theory* focuses our attention on how certain behaviors are linked to, or contained by, our genes.
4.	T	F	One of the *social foundations of deviance* is that deviance exists only in relation to cultural norms.
5.	T	F	In Robert Merton's *strain theory* the concept deviance is applied by linking deviance to certain social imbalances between *goals* and *means*.
6.	T	F	Walter Miller's *subcultural theory* of deviance points out that deviant subcultures have *no focal concerns*, and therefore have no social norms to guide the behavior of their members.
7.	T	F	*Primary deviance* tends to be more harmful to society than *secondary deviance*.
8.	T	F	Thomas Szaz argues that *mental illness* is a *myth* and is a label used by the powerful in society to force people to follow dominant cultural norms.
9.	T	F	Our author suggests that during the last fifty years there has been a trend away from what is known as the *medicalization of deviance*.
10.	T	F	Edwin Sutherland's *differential association theory* suggests that certain individuals are incapable of learning from experience and therefore are more likely to become deviant.
11.	T	F	The *social-conflict* perspective links deviance to social inequality and power in society.
12.	T	F	What qualifies an offense as a *hate crime* is not so much a matter of the race or ancestry of the victim as it is the *motivation* of the offender.
13.	T	F	According to the FBI's "Index Crimes," robbery and murder are examples of *violent crime*.

14.   T   F   Using *index crimes*, the crime rate in the United States is relatively high compared to European societies.

15.   T   F   *Plea Bargaining* account for about forty percent of criminal cases resolved by the courts.

16.   T   F   *Criminal recidivism*, while relatively high historically in the United States, has in recent years shown a significant decline.

Multiple Choice

1. _____ refers to the recognized violation of cultural norms.

     (a)   Crime
     (b)   Deviance
     (c)   Residual behavior
     (d)   Social control
     (e)   Law

2. *Containment theory* is an example of a(n) _____ explanation of deviance.

     (a)   biological
     (b)   psychological
     (c)   anthropological
     (d)   sociological

3. Which of the following is *not a social foundation* of deviance?

     (a)   Deviance exists in relation to cultural norms.
     (b)   People become deviant in that others define them that way.
     (c)   Both norms and the way people define social situations involve social power.
     (d)   All are identified as foundations of deviance.

4. *Emile Durkheim* theorized that all but which of the following are *functions of deviance*?

     (a)   it clarifies moral boundaries.
     (b)   it affirms cultural values and norms.
     (c)   it encourages social stability.
     (d)   it promotes social unity.

5. *Robert Merton's stain theory* is a component of which broad theoretical paradigm?

     (a)   social-conflict
     (b)   symbolic-interactionism
     (c)   social-exchange
     (d)   human ecology
     (e)   structural-functional

6. Which of the following is *not* an example of a *deviant subculture* identified in *Richard Cloward* and *Lloyd Olhin's* research on delinquents.

   (a) criminal
   (b) retreatist
   (c) conflict
   (d) residual

7. Which of the following theories is *not derived* from the *structural-functional paradigm*?

   (a) labeling theory
   (b) strain theory
   (c) deviant subculture theory
   (d) control theory

8. Which of the following is an appropriate criticism of *structural-functional theories* of deviance?

   (a) The theories assume a diversity of cultural standards.
   (b) The theories assume a single cultural standard.
   (c) The theories focus on the lower-class.
   (d) The theories overplay the importance of societal definitions of deviance.

9. Which theory asserts that deviance and conformity result from the responses of others?

   (a) differential association
   (b) social conflict
   (c) labeling
   (d) structural-functionalism

10. Skipping school for the first time as an eighth grader is an example of:

    (a) recidivism.
    (b) primary deviance.
    (c) a degradation ceremony.
    (d) secondary deviance.

11. What is Erving Goffman's term for a powerful negative social label that radically changes a person's self-concept and social identity?

    (a) anomie
    (b) secondary deviance
    (c) medicalization of deviance
    (d) retribution
    (e) stigma

12. Sometimes an entire community formally stigmatizes an individual through what *Harold Garfinkel* called a:

(a) hate crime.
(b) retrospective label
(c) recidivism process.
(d) degradation ceremony.
(e) conflict subculture.

13. What is the *medicalization of deviance*?

(a) the recognition of the true source of deviance
(b) the objective, clinical approach to deviant behavior
(c) the transformation of moral and legal issues into medical models
(d) the discovery of the links between biochemical properties and deviance

14. *Attachment, involvement, commitment,* and *belief* are all types of social control in:

(a) Suteherland's differential association theory.
(b) Durkheim's functional theory.
(c) Goffman's labeling theory.
(d) Cohen's subcultural theory.
(e) Hirschi's control theory.

15. According to the *social-conflict paradigm*, who and what is labeled deviant is based primarily on:

(a) the severity of the deviant act.
(b) psychological profile.
(c) the functions being served.
(d) relative power.

16. What is the term for crime committed by persons of high social position in the course of their occupations.

(a) occupational crimes
(b) status offenses
(c) white-collar crime
(d) residual crime

17. The statements: While what is deviant may vary, deviance itself is found in all societies. Deviance and the social response it provokes serve to maintain the moral foundation of society. Deviance can direct social change. All help to summarize which sociological explanation of deviance?

    (a)   structural-functional
    (b)   social-conflict
    (c)   symbolic-interaction
    (d)   labeling
    (e)   social exchange

18. Which contribution below is attributed to the *structural-functional theory* of deviance?

    (a)   Nothing is inherently deviant.
    (b)   Deviance is found in all societies.
    (c)   The reactions of others to deviance are highly variable.
    (d)   Laws and other norms reflect the interests of the powerful in society.

19. Which of the following are included as part of the FBI *index crimes*?

    (a)   white-collar crime and property crime
    (b)   victimless crime and federal crime
    (c)   crime against the state and civil crime
    (d)   crime against the person and crime against property
    (e)   violent crime and white-collar crime

20. Which of the following is *not listed* as a *justification for punishment* in our criminal justice system?

    (a)   retribution
    (b)   societal protection
    (c)   deterrence
    (d)   rehabilitation
    (e)   all of the above are justifications

Matching

1. ____   According to Robert Merton's *strain theory*, these are different ways of responding to the inability to succeed through conformity.
2. ____   The assertion that deviance and conformity result, not so much from what people do, as from how others respond to those actions.
3. ____   Violations of law in which there are no apparent victims.
4. ____   Types of *social controls* according to Travis Hirschi.
5. ____   Crime in the *suites*.
6. ____   Types of *deviant subcultures* identified by Richard Cloward and Lloyd Ohlin's theory of relative opportunity structure.

7. ____ A legal negotiation in which the prosecution reduces a charge in exchange for a defendant's guilty plea.
8. ____ The recognized violation of cultural norms.
9. ____ Attempts by society to regulate behavior people's thought and behavior.
10. ____ A powerfully negative label that radically changes a person's self-concept and social identity.

a. criminal, conflict, retreatist
b. victimless crime
c. plea bargaining
d. labeling theory
e. deviance

f. attachment, involvement, belief, commitment
g. stigma
h. social control
i. retreatism, rebellion, ritualism, innovation
j. white collar crime

Fill-In

1. _____ is the violation of norms a society formally enacts into criminal law.
2. The _____ _____ _____ is the formal response to alleged violations of law on the part of police, courts, and prison officials.
3. *William Sheldon* argued that _____ might predict criminality.
4. A *psychological explanation* of deviance that posits the view that if boys have developed strong moral values and a positive self-image they will not become delinquents is called _____ theory.
5. The *social foundations of deviance* include: Deviance varies according to _____ _____; People become deviant as others _____ them that way; And, both norms and the way people define situations involve social _____.
6. The *strain theory* of deviance is based on the _____ *paradigm*.
7. *Richard Cloward* and *Lloyd Ohlin* explain deviance and conformity in terms of the _____ _____ structure young people face in their lives.
8. Activity that is initially defined as deviant is called _____ *deviance*. On the other hand, a person who accepts the label of deviant may then engage in _____ *deviance*, or behavior caused by the person's incorporating the deviant label into their self-concept.
9. Psychiatrist Thomas Szaz argues that *mental illness* is a _____.
10. Travis Hirschi links *conformity* to four types of social control, including _____, _____, _____, and _____.
11. *Social-conflict theory* demonstrates that deviance reflects *social* _____. This approach suggests that *who* or *what* is labeled as deviant is based largely on the relative _____ of categories of people.
12. _____ *crime* is defined as crimes committed by persons of high social position in the course of their occupations.
13. _____ *law* refers to general regulations involving economic affairs between private parties.
14. _____ *surveys* show that the actual level of crime is three times as great as that indicated by official reports.
15. The *criminal justice system* in the U.S. consists of three elements: _____, _____, and _____.

16.	The four basic *justifications for punishment* include: _____, _____, _____, and _____ _____.
17.	Subsequent offenses by people previously convicted of crimes is termed *criminal* _____.
18.	According to Travis Hirschi, the two key characteristics that define the population of *criminal offenders* are _____ and _____.

Definition and Short-Answer

1.	According to *Travis Hirschi's control theory* there are four types of social controls. What are these? Provide an example of each.
2.	According to *Robert Merton's strain theory*, what are the four deviant responses by individuals to dominant cultural patterns when there is a gap between *means* and *goals*? Provide an illustration of each.
3.	According to *Emile Durkheim*, what are the *functions of deviance*? Provide an illustration for each .
4.	*Social-conflict* theorist *Steven Spitzer* argues that deviant labels are applied to people who impede the operation of *capitalism*. What are the four reasons he gives for this phenomenon?
5.	How do researchers using *differential association theory* explain deviance?
6.	What is meant by the term *medicalization of deviance*? Provide two illustrations.
7.	According to *Elliot Currie*, what factors are responsible for the relatively high crime rates in the United States?
8.	What are the four *justifications* for the use of punishment against criminals? What evidence exists for their relative effectiveness?
9.	*Richard Cloward* and *Lloyd Ohlin* investigated delinquent youth and explain deviance and conformity in terms of the *relative opportunity structure* young people face in their lives. Identify and define the three types of *subcultures* these researchers have identified as representing the criminal lifestyles of delinquent youth.
10.	Describe *Thomas Szaz's* view of mental illness and deviance. Your opinions of his arguments?
11.	Briefly review the demographic *profile* of the *street criminal*.
12.	Critique the official statistics of crime in the United States. What are the weaknesses of the measures used in the identification of *crime rates*?
13.	What are the three consequences for the deviant person depending on whether a *moral model* or *medical model* is applied?

PART VI: ANSWERS TO STUDY QUESTIONS

True-False

1.	T	(p. 132)	9.	F	(p. 138)
2.	F	(p. 133)	10.	F	(p. 139)
3.	F	(p. 133)	11.	T	(p. 140)
4.	T	(p. 133)	12.	T	(p. 143)
5.	T	(p. 135)	13.	T	(p. 145)
6.	F	(p. 136)	14.	T	(p. 147)
7.	F	(p. 137)	15.	F	(p. 152)
8.	T	(p. 138)	16.	F	(p. 154)

Multiple Choice

1.	b	(p. 131)	11.	e	(p. 137)
2.	b	(p. 133)	12.	d	(p. 137)
3.	d	(pp. 133-134)	13.	c	(p. 138)
4.	c	(pp. 133-134)	14.	e	(pp. 139-140)
5.	e	(p. 135)	15.	d	(p. 141)
6.	d	(p. 136)	16.	c	(p. 142)
7.	a	(p. 137)	17.	a	(p. 143)
8.	b	(p. 137)	18.	b	(p. 143)
9.	c	(p. 137)	19.	d	(p. 145)
10.	b	(p. 137)	20.	e	(pp. 152-153)

Matching

1.	i	(p. 135)	6.	a	(p. 136)
2.	d	(p. 137)	7.	c	(p. 152)
3.	b	(p. 146)	8.	e	(p. 131)
4.	f	(pp. 139-140)	9.	h	(p. 132)
5.	j	(p. 142)	10.	g	(p. 137)

Fill-In

1. Crime (p. 131)
2. criminal justice system (p. 132)
3. body structure (p. 132)
4. containment (p. 133)
5. cultural norms, define, power (pp. 133-134)
6. structural-functional (p. 135)
7. relative opportunity (p. 136)
8. primary, secondary (p. 137)
9. myth (p. 138)
10. attachment, commitment, involvement, belief (pp. 139-140)
11. inequality, power (p. 140)
12. white-collar (p. 142)
13. civil (p. 142)
14. victimization (p. 146)
15. police, courts, punishment (p. 151)
16. retribution, deterrence, rehabilitation, societal protection (pp. 152-153)
17. recidivism (p. 154)
18. age, low self-control (p. 155)

PART VII: IN FOCUS—MAJOR ISSUE

- Emile Durkheim suggested deviance performs four essential *functions*. What are these? Provide an illustration for each.

- Robert Merton argued that excessive deviance arises from particular social arrangements. What is his theory called? What does his theory tell us about the relationship between *means* and *goals* in society? Provide an example for each of the *responses to strain* identified in Merton's theory.

  Responses: conformity, innovation, ritualism, retreatist, rebellion

- Walter Miller suggests that *deviant subcultures* are characterized by:

- Identify the major concepts and ideas related each of the following theories associated with the *symbolic-interaction approach*.

  Labeling theory:

Differential association theory:

Control theory:

- The *social- conflict approach* links deviance to social inequality. What do proponents of these approaches suggest about the following:

  Deviance and power:

  Deviance and capitalism:

- What do the government crime reports tell us about the following demographic characteristics of people arrested for *violent* and *property* crime?

  Age: Gender:

  Social class: Race:

- Describe each of the following *components of the criminal justice system.*

  Police:

  Courts:

  Punishment:

- Define each of the following four *justifications for punishment.*

Retribution: Deterrence:

Rehabilitation: Societal Protection:

PART VIII: ANALYSIS AND COMMENT

Critical Thinking

"Date Rape: Exposing Dangerous Myths"

Key Points: Questions:

Controversy and Debate

"What Can Be Done About Crime?"

Key Points: Questions:

94

Window on the World--Global Map 6-1

"Prostitution in Global Perspective"

Key Points: Questions:

Seeing Ourselves--National Map 6-1 and 6-2

"Where Psychiatrists Practice Across the United States"

Key Points: Questions:

"Capital Punishment across the United States"

Key Points: Questions:

Social Stratification

PART I: CHAPTER OUTLINE

I. What is Social Stratification
II. Caste and Class Systems
    A.   The Caste System
    B.   The Class System
    C.   Ideology: Stratification's "Staying Power"
III. The Functions of Social Stratification
    A.   The Davis-Moore Thesis
IV. Stratification and Conflict
    A.   Karl Marx: Class Conflict
    B.   Why No Marxist Revolution?
    C.   Max Weber: Class, Status, and Power
V. Stratification and Technology: A Global Perspective
VI. Inequality In the United States
    A.   Income, Wealth, and Power
    B.   Occupational Prestige
    C.   Schooling
    D.   Ancestry, Race, and Gender
VII. Social Classes in the United States
    A.   The Upper Class
    B.   The Middle Class
    C.   The Working Class
    D.   The Lower Class
VIII. The Difference Class Makes
    A.   Health
    B.   Values and Attitudes
    C.   Family Patterns
IX. Social Mobility
    A.   Myth Versus Reality
    B.   Mobility by Income Level
    C.   Mobility by Race, Ethnicity, and Gender
    D.   The American Dream: Still a Reality?
    E.   The Global Economy and the U.S. Class Structure

PART II: LEARNING OBJECTIVES

1. To understand the four basic principles of social stratification.
2. To be able to differentiate between the caste and class system of stratification.
3. To begin to understand the relationship between ideology and stratification.
4. To be able to differentiate between the structural-functional and social-conflict perspectives of stratification.
5. To be able to describe the views of Max Weber concerning the dimensions of social class.
6. To be able to describe the approach to understanding social stratification as presented by the Lenskis.
7. To develop a sense about the extent of social inequality in the United States.
8. To consider the meaning of the concept of socioeconomic status and to be aware of its dimensions.
9. To be able to review the role of economic resources, power and occupational prestige, and schooling in the U.S. class system.
10. To be able to identify and trace the significance of various ascribed statuses for the construction and maintenance of social stratification in the United States.
11. To begin to see the significance of the global economy and its impact on our economic system.
12. To be able to generally describe the various social classes in our social stratification system.
13. To become aware of how health, values, and family life are related to the social-class system in our society.
14. To begin to develop a sociological understanding about the nature of social mobility in the United States.
15. To develop a general understanding of the demographics of poverty in the United States.
16. To become aware and critical of different explanations of poverty.
17. To develop an awareness of the problem of homelessness in the United States.
18. To consider some of the dilemmas involved in public assistance and welfare reform.

PART III: KEY CONCEPTS

absolute poverty
alienation
blue-collar occupation
capitalists
caste system
class system
culture of poverty

Davis-Moore thesis
Endogamous
femininization of poverty
horizontal social mobility
ideology
income
intergenerational social mobility
intragenerational social mobility
Kuznets curve
lower-class
marginal poor
meritocracy
middle-class
occupational prestige
perestroika
primogeniture
proletariat
relative poverty
social inequality
social mobility
social stratification
socioeconomic status
status consistency
structural social mobility
upper-class
wealth
white-collar occupation

PART IV: IMPORTANT RESEARCHERS

Karl Marx   Max Weber

Gerhard and Jean Lenski   Plato

Melvin Tumin   Ralph Darendorf

William Julius Wilson   Edward Banfield

Oscar Lewis

PART V: STUDY QUESTIONS

<u>True-False</u>

1.	T	F	Social inequality is *universal*--found in all societies.
2.	T	F	*Ascription* is fundamental to social-stratification systems based on *castes*.
3.	T	F	*Caste* systems tend to be characterized by *endogamous marriages*.
4.	T	F	The *working class* is the largest segment of the population in *Great Britain*.
5.	T	F	*Ideology* refers to cultural beliefs that serve to justify social stratification.
6.	T	F	The ancient Greek philosopher *Plato* defined *justice* as agreement about who should have what.
7.	T	F	The *Davis-Moore thesis* is a component of the social-conflict perspective of social stratification.
8.	T	F	*Structural-functionalists* argue that social stratification encourages a matching of talents and abilities to appropriate positions in society.
9.	T	F	*Karl Marx's* social conflict theory of social stratification identified two basic relationships to the means of production--those who own productive property, and those labor for others.
10.	T	F	Unlike Karl Marx, *Max Weber* believed that socialism would increase inequality by expanding government and concentrating power in the hands of political elite.
11.	T	F	*Gerhard* and *Jean Lenski* argue that hunting and gathering societies have greater social inequality than agrarian or horticultural societies.
12.	T	F	The *Kutznets curve* projects greater social inequality as industrial societies advance technologically.
13.	T	F	*Wealth* in the United States is distributed more equally than income.
14.	T	F	*Wealth* is defined as the total value of money and other assets, minus outstanding debts.
15.	T	F	Recent government calculations place the wealth of the average U.S. household at about $40,000.
16.	T	F	Only about sixty-five percent of adults in the U.S. have a high school diploma.
17.	T	F	Only slightly more than twenty percent of U.S. adults have a college degree.
18.	T	F	The *working class* is the largest social class in the United States.
19.	T	F	Parents in *working-class* families are characterized by an emphasis on *conformity* to conventional beliefs and practices, more so than are middle- class families.

99

20.	T	F	The *middle-class slide* is an example of downward structural mobility.
21.	T	F	Compared to the period of 1950-1973, the period 1974-1995 provided greater growth in *median family income*, particularly with more dual earner families in existence.
22.	T	F	The official *poverty rate* in the United States in 1996 was approximately 13.7 percent.
23.	T	F	The *poverty threshold* is three times what the government estimates people must spend to eat.
24.	T	F	Two-thirds of all poor people in the U.S. are African American.
25.	T	F	The poverty rate among the elderly in the U.S. is higher than the rate for children.
26.	T	F	The *culture of poverty* is a concept relating poverty to a lower-class subculture that inhibits personal achievement and foster resignation.
27.	T	F	William Julius Wilson believes that the solution to the problems of inner cities is the *creation of jobs*.
28.	T	F	Among the poor in the U.S., over sixty percent of the heads of households are employed *full-time*.
29.	T	F	People in the U.S. are more likely to blame individuals rather than society for poverty compared to people in other industrialized societies.
30.	T	F	Welfare reform over the last couple of years has reduced the nation's welfare rolls by about forty percent.

Multiple Choice

1. A system by which a society ranks categories of people in a hierarchy is called:

    (a)   social inequality.
    (b)   meritocracy.
    (c)   social stratification.
    (d)   social mobility.

2. Which of the following principles is *not* a basic factor in explaining the existence of social stratification?

    (a)   Although universal, social stratification also varies in form.
    (b)   Social stratification persists over generations.
    (c)   Social stratification rests on widely held beliefs.
    (d)   Social stratification is a characteristic of society, not simply a function of individual differences.
    (e)   All are factors in explaining social stratification.

3. A change in one's position in a social hierarchy refers to:

    (a)   ideology.
    (b)   social mobility.
    (c)   meritocracy.
    (d)   social inequality.
    (e)   endogamy.

4. What is a *caste system*?

   (a) social stratification based on ascription
   (b) social stratification based on meritocracy
   (c) social stratification based on achievement
   (d) any system in which there is social inequality

5. *Apartheid* became law in South Africa in:

   (a) 1916.
   (b) 1971.
   (c) 1948.
   (d) 1876.

6. Which characteristics that follow are most accurate of *class systems*?

   (a) they are more clearly defined than castes
   (b) they have variable status consistency
   (c) they have occupations based on ascription
   (d) all of the above

7. What is the term for the degree of consistency in a person's social standing across various dimensions of social inequality?

   (a) status consonance
   (b) status congruity
   (c) status balance
   (d) status consistency
   (e) socioeconomic status

8. In the Middle Ages, social stratification in England was a system of three _____.

   (a) open classes
   (b) absolute castes
   (c) meritocracies
   (d) closed classes
   (e) caste-like estates

9. The social stratification system in Great Britain today still has vestiges of its feudal system of the past. Which of the following was characteristic of their feudal system?

   (a) It was a caste-like estate system.
   (b) It was based on the law of primogeniture.
   (c) It consisted of the nobility, the clergy, and the commoners.
   (d) all of the above

10. Contemporary *Great Britain* is identified as a(n):

    (a)   neomonarchy.
    (b)   caste system.
    (c)   estate system.
    (d)   open estate system.
    (e)   class society.

11. Which of the following comprises one-half of all persons in contemporary Great Britain?

    (a)   working class
    (b)   upper class
    (c)   lower class
    (d)   middle class

12. The former Soviet Union had four levels in their social stratification system. The highest level was known as:

    (a)   intelligentsia.
    (b)   perestroika.
    (c)   apparatchiks.
    (d)   primogeniture.
    (e)   nogoodniks.

13. What is *ideology*?

    (a)   a system in which entire categories of people are ranked in a hierarchy
    (b)   ideas that are generated through scientific investigation
    (c)   views and opinions that are based on the principle of cultural relativism
    (d)   ideas that limit the amount of inequality of a society
    (e)   cultural beliefs that serve to justify social stratification

14. The *Davis-Moore thesis* asserts that:

    (a)   social stratification has beneficial consequences for the operation of society.
    (b)   industrialization produces greater, and more harmful social stratification than previous forms of subsistence.
    (c)   social stratification based on meritocracy has dysfunctional consequences for society and its individual members.
    (d)   ideology undermines social stratification.
    (e)   industrial capitalism is moving toward a classless social order.

15. Which perspective of social stratification views social inequality as the domination of some categories of people by others?

    (a)   symbolic-interactionism
    (b)   sociocultural evolution
    (c)   social-conflict
    (d)   structural-functionalism

16. In Karl Marx's analysis of social stratification, another name for the working class is the:

    (a)   primogeniture.
    (b)   perestroika.
    (c)   apparatchiks.
    (d)   proletariat.
    (e)   bourgeoisie.

17. Which of the following is/are reasons given as to why there has been *no Marxist revolution*?

    (a)   the fragmentation of the capitalist class
    (b)   a higher standard of living
    (c)   more extensive worker organization
    (d)   more extensive legal protections
    (e)   all of the above

18. Which of the following is not one of the dimensions of social stratification according to Max Weber?

    (a)   class
    (b)   socioeconomic status
    (c)   power
    (d)   status

19. According to the model of *sociocultural evolution* developed by *Gerhard* and *Jean Lenski*, social stratification is at its peak in:

    (a)   hunting and gathering societies.
    (b)   postindustrial societies.
    (c)   large-scale agrarian societies.
    (d)   industrial societies.

20. The *Kuznet's curve* suggests:

    (a)   industrialization and social stratification are unrelated.
    (b)   industrial societies, in the long run, will become more stratified.
    (c)   industrial societies tend to become less stratified over time.
    (d)   status inconsistency and meritocracy created greater inequality in modern postindustrial society as compared to earlier periods of industrialization.

21. Census Bureau data show that *income* and *wealth* are unequally distributed in the United States. Which of the following statements is most accurate?

    (a)   The median household income in the U.S. in 1997 was $63,036.
    (b)   The top five percent of households (by income) receive sixty-five percent of the income earned in the U.S.
    (c)   The poorest twenty percent of households only receive ten percent of the income earned in the U.S.
    (d)   Wealth is distributed more unequally in the U.S. than is income.

22. *Education* is distributed unequally in the U.S. as evidenced by the fact that:

    (a)   only a little more than twenty percent of the adult population has a college education.
    (b)   only about fifty-five percent of the adult population has a high school education.
    (c)   thirty percent of adults have not completed high school.
    (d)   all of the above

23. In 1996, African American families earned _____ percent of that earned by white families.

    (a)   90
    (b)   80
    (c)   73
    (d)   52
    (e)   61

24. African American households have an average *wealth* that is _____ of white households.

    (a)   one-half
    (b)   one-third
    (c)   one-tenth
    (d)   one-fifth
    (e)   three-quarters

25. The *middle class* includes approximately what percentage of the U.S. population?

    (a)   20-25
    (b)   40-45
    (c)   30-35
    (d)   55-60

26. Which of the following statements is/are accurate regarding general patterns in our society?

    (a) Working-class parents tend to encourage children to conform to conventional norms and obey and respect authority.
    (b) Middle-class parents tend to teach children to express their individuality.
    (c) Most working-class couples divide their responsibilities according to gender.
    (d) Middle-class couples tend to be more egalitarian than working-class couples.
    (e) all of the above

27. What does research reveal about *social mobility* in the United States?

    (a) Social mobility, at least among men, has been relatively low.
    (b) The long-term trend in social mobility has been downward.
    (c) Within a single generation, social mobility is usually dramatic, not incremental.
    (d) The short-term trend has been stagnation, with some income polarization.

28. A change in social position of children relative to that of their parents is called:

    (a) horizontal social mobility.
    (b) structural social mobility.
    (c) intergenerational social mobility.
    (d) intragenerational social mobility.

29. What evidence exists that there is *income stagnation* in our society in recent years?

    (a) For many workers, earnings have stalled.
    (b) Multiple-job holding is up.
    (c) More jobs offer little income.
    (d) more young people are remaining at home.
    (e) all of the above

30. High-paying jobs in *manufacturing* accounted for twenty-six percent of jobs in 1960, today, such jobs support _____ percent of our workforce.

    (a) 30
    (b) 16
    (c) 25
    (d) 4
    (e) 10

31. Approximately what percentage of the U.S. population is officially classified as being poor?

    (a) 5
    (b) 13
    (c) 19
    (d) 26
    (e) 31

105

32. Poverty statistics in the United States reveal that:

    (a)   the elderly are more likely than any other age group to be poor.
    (b)   almost 70 percent of all African Americans are poor.
    (c)   urban and suburban poverty rates are considerably higher than rural poverty rates.
    (d)   about 63 percent of the poor adults are female.

33. The *culture of poverty* view concerning the causes of poverty:

    (a)   holds that the poor are primarily responsible for their own poverty.
    (b)   blames poverty on economic stagnation relating to the globalization of the U.S. economy.
    (c)   sees lack of ambition on the part of the poor as a consequence, not a cause for poverty.
    (d)   views the conservative economic policies of the last two decades in the U.S. as the primary reason for relatively high poverty rates.

Matching

1. ____ The total value of money and other assets, minus outstanding debts.
2. ____ Encompasses 40 to 45 percent of the U.S. population and exerts a tremendous influence on U.S. culture.
3. ____ Accounts for about one-third of the U.S. population.
4. ____ A change in social position occurring within a person's lifetime.
5. ____ Upward or downward social mobility of children in relation to their parents.
6. ____ A form of downward structural social mobility.
7. ____ The deprivation of some people in relation to those who have more.
8. ____ Describes the trend by which women represent an increasing proportion of the poor.
9. ____ Developed the concept of the *culture of poverty*, or a lower-class subculture that inhibits personal achievement and fosters resignation to one's plight.
10. ____ Argued that *society* is primarily responsible for poverty and that any lack of ambition on the part of the poor is a *consequence* of insufficient opportunity.
11. ____ According to Karl Marx, the people who own and operate factories and other productive businesses in pursuit of profit.
12. ____ The assertion that social stratification is universal because it has beneficial consequences for the operation of society.
13. ____ The degree of consistency in a person's social standing across various dimensions of social inequality.
14. ____ According to Karl Marx, the people who sell their productive labor for wages.
15. ____ Social stratification based on *ascription*.
16. ____ Cultural beliefs that justify social stratification.
17. ____ Reveals that greater *technological* sophistication is generally accompanied by more pronounced *social stratification*, to a point.
18. ____ Developed a *multidimensional model* of social class which included the variables of *class, status,* and *power*.
19. ____ An economic program, meaning *restructuring*, developed by Mikhail Gorbachev.
20. ____ The experience of *powerlessness* in social life.

a.	William Julius Wilson	k.	ideology
b.	intergenerational social mobility	l.	capitalists
c.	femininization of poverty	m.	the Davis-Moore thesis
d.	wealth	n.	status consistency
e.	intragenertional social mobility	o.	perestroika
f.	the working- class	p.	caste
g.	Oscar Lewis	q.	Kuznets curve
h.	The middle-class	r.	Max Weber
i.	The middle-class slide	s.	proletariat
j.	Relative poverty	t.	alienation

Fill-In

1. *Social* _____ refers to a system by which a society ranks categories of people in a hierarchy.

2. Social stratification is a matter of four *basic principles*: It is a characteristic of _____, not simply a reflection of individual differences; It _____ over generations; I is _____ but variable; And, it involves not just inequality but _____.

3. Caste systems mandate that people marry others of the same ranking. Sociologists call this pattern _____ *marriage*.

4. Whereas a _____ is a system of social stratification based on *ascription*, a _____ is a system in which social position is based entirely on *personal merit*..

5. In feudal Great Britain, the *law of* _____ mandated that only the eldest son inherited property of parents.

6. _____ *social mobility* refers to a shift in the social position of large numbers of people due more to changes in society itself than to individual efforts.

7. _____ refers to cultural beliefs that justify social stratification.

8. According to *Karl Marx*, capitalism produces _____, or the experience of *powerlessness* in social life.

9. Four reasons are given as to why there has been *no Marxist revolution*, including: The _____ of the capitalist class, a _____ standard of living, more extensive worker _____, and more extensive legal _____.

10. Advocates of *social-conflict analysis* believe that Karl Marx's analysis of capitalism is still largely valid. They offer the following reasons: Wealth remains largely _____, _____ work offers little to workers, progress requires _____. the _____ still favors the rich.

11. The three components of *Max Weber's* model of social class are _____, _____, and _____.

12. _____ *status* refers to a composite ranking based on various dimensions of social inequality.

13. Gerhard and Jean Lenski argue that the level of _____ representative of a society

14. In 1997, the richest twenty percent of families in the U.S. control _____ percent of all *income*.

15. _____ is the total value of money and other assets, minus outstanding debts.
16. When financial assets are balanced against debits, the lowest-ranking _____ percent of U.S. families have virtually no *wealth* at all.
17. The *median family income* for African Americans in 1997 was _____.
18. The *working-class* comprises about _____ percent of the U.S. population.
19. In 1997, the federal government classified _____ of our population as *poor*.
20. While the relationship between social class and politics is complex, generally, members of high social standing tend to have _____ *views on economic issues* and _____ *views on social issues.*
21. _____ *social mobility* refers to a change in social position occurring within a person's lifetime.
22. Evidence of "income stagnation" in our society today includes: For many workers, earnings have _____, _____ job-holding is up, more jobs offer little _____, and young people are remaining _____.
23. _____ *poverty* refers to deprivation of some people in relation to those who have more.
24. For an urban family of four, in 1997, the poverty threshold was _____.
25. _____ of the poor are *elderly people.*
26. The trend by which females represent an increasing proportion of the poor is called the _____ *of poverty.*
27. In the United States in 1997, _____ of *children* were poor.
28. According to William Julius Wilson sees any apparent lack of ambition on the part of the poor as a _____ of insufficient opportunity rather than a _____ of poverty.
29. Virtually all *homeless people* have one status in common: _____.
30. *Conservatives* believe government assistance undermines _____ among the poor, and erodes the traditional _____.
31. More of the U.S. population attributes poverty to personal _____ than _____.
32. Welfare reform has included replacing the federal AFDC program with TANF or _____ _____, a program with funding for new state-run programs.

Definition and Short-Answer

1. What are the four *fundamental principles* of social stratification?
2. Briefly describe the social-stratification system of *Great Britain.*
3. What are the four reasons given in the text for why the *Marxist Revolution* has not occurred?
4. What are the basic qualities of a *caste system*?
5. What is meant by the concept *structural social mobility*? Provide two illustrations.
6. What are the components of *Max Weber's* multidimensional model of social stratification? Define each.
7. What are three criteria of the *Davis-Moore thesis*? What is your opinion of this thesis and its relevance for helping us understand our social stratification? What evidence exists in support of this thesis? What evidence contradicts it?
8. How are *wealth* and *income* distributed throughout the population in the United States?
9. What are the basic components of *socioeconomic status*? How are they measured? How do these components differ from Max Weber's components of social class?

10. To what extent do *ascribed statuses* affect a person's place in our social-stratification system? Provide examples using the variables of race, ethnicity, and gender.

11. Using the factors of health, values, and politics, discuss the difference social class makes in the lives of people within our society.

12. Identify six significant *demographic characteristics* of the poor in our society today.

13. What is meant by the term *culture of poverty*? What policies and programs do you think could be instituted to counteract this phenomenon?

14. What is meant by the terms *femininization of poverty*? What can be done to reverse this trend in our society?

15. Review the basic points being made by *Gerhard* and *Jean Lenski* concerning global inequality in historical perspective.

16. What is the evidence that the *American Dream* is waning in our society?

PART VI: ANSWERS TO STUDY QUESTIONS

True-False

1.	T	(p. 162)	16.	F	(p. 177)
2.	T	(p. 162)	17.	T	(p. 179)
3.	T	(p. 163)	18.	F	(p. 180)
4.	T	(p. 166)	19.	T	(p. 182)
5.	T	(p. 168)	20.	T	(p. 184)
6.	T	(p. 168)	21.	F	(p. 185)
7.	F	(p. 169)	22.	T	(p. 186)
8.	T	(p. 169)	23.	T	(p. 186)
9.	T	(pp. 170-171)	24.	F	(p. 186)
10.	T	(p. 173)	25.	F	(p. 186)
11.	T	(p. 174)	26.	T	(p. 187)
12.	F	(p. 174)	27.	T	(p. 188)
13.	F	(p. 176)	28.	F	(p. 188)
14.	T	(p. 176)	29.	T	(p. 189)
15.	T	(p. 177)	30.	T	(p. 191)

Multiple-Choice

1.	c	(p. 162)	18.	b	(p. 172)
2.	e	(p. 162)	19.	c	(p. 174)
3.	b	(p. 162)	20.	c	(p. 174)
4.	a	(p. 162)	21.	d	(p. 176)
5.	c	(p. 164)	22.	a	(p. 177)
6.	b	(p. 164)	23.	e	(p. 178)
7.	d	(p. 164)	24.	c	(p. 179)
8.	e	(p. 165)	25.	b	(p. 180)
9.	d	(p. 165)	26.	e	(p. 180)
10.	e	(p. 166)	27.	d	(p. 183)

11.	a	(p. 166)		28.	c	(p. 183)
12.	c	(p. 166)		29.	e	(p. 184)
13.	e	(p. 168)		30.	b	(p. 185)
14.	a	(p. 169)		31.	b	(p. 186)
15.	c	(p. 170)		32.	d	(p. 186)
16.	d	(p. 171)		33.	a	(p. 187)
17.	e	(pp. 171-172)				

Matching

1.	d	(p. 176)		11.	l	(p. 171)
2.	h	(p. 180)		12.	m	(p. 169)
3.	f	(p. 180)		13.	n	(p. 164)
4.	e	(pp. 182-183)		14.	s	(p. 171)
5.	b	(p. 183)		15.	p	(p. 162)
6.	I	(p. 184)		16.	k	(p. 168)
7.	j	(p. 185)		17.	q	(p. 174)
8.	c	(p. 186)		18.	r	(p. 172)
9.	g	(p. 187)		19.	o	(p. 162)
10.	a	(p. 188)		20.	t	(p. 171)

Fill-In

1. stratification (p. 162)
2. society, persists, universal, beliefs (p. 162)
3. endogamous (p. 163)
4. caste, meritocracy (p. 163)
5. primogeniture (p. 165)
6. structural (p. 167)
7. ideology (p. 168)
8. alienation (p. 171)
9. fragmentation, higher, organization, protection (pp. 171-172)
10. concentrated, white-collar, struggle, law (p. 172)
11. class, status, power (p. 172)
12. socioeconomic (pp. 172-173)
13. technology (p. 173)
14. 47.2 (p. 176)
15. wealth (p. 176)
16. 40 (p. 177)
17. $28,602 (p. 178)
18. 33 (p. 180)
19. 13.3 (p. 180)
20. conservative, liberal (p. 182)
21. intragenerational (p. 183)
22. stalled, multiple, income, home (p. 184)

23.   relative (p. 185)
24. $16,400 (p. 186)
25.   10.5 (p. 186)
26.   femininization (p. 186)
27.   19.9 (p. 186)
28.   consequences, cause (p. 188)
29.   poverty (p. 189)
30.   laziness, societal injustice (p. 189)
31.   self-reliance, family (p. 190)
32.   temporary assistance for needy families (p. 191)

PART VII: IN FOCUS—MAJOR ISSUES

- What is *social stratification*? What are the four *basic principles* of social stratification?

- Identify the basic characteristics of the following types of social stratification systems:

    Caste: Class:

- What is the *Davis-Moore thesis*? What do critics argue about this structural-functional view of social stratification?

- What is *Karl Marx's* view of social stratification in a capitalist class system?

- What are the three dimensions of social class according to *Max Weber*?

- Provide evidence of social inequality in the U.S. for the following variable—making specific references to *Figure 7-3, 7-4, and Table 7-2.*

    Income:

    Wealth:

- Identify 3-4 general characteristics for each of the following *social classes*.

  The Upper Class:

  The Middle Class:

  The Working Class:

  The Lower Class:

- Briefly describe how class *makes a difference* in the following domains of life.

  Health:

  Values and Attitudes:

  Family Patterns:

- What are the four general conclusions about *social mobility* in the United States being made in the text?

- What are the four pieces of evidence given in the text for a slowing in upward social mobility in the United States?

- Who are the *poor*? (general demographic patterns)

    Age: Gender and Family Patterns:

    Race and Ethnicity: Urban and Rural Poverty:

PART VIII: ANALYSIS AND COMMENT

Global Sociology

"Race as caste: A Report from South Africa"

Key Points: Questions:

Critical Thinking

"Is Getting Rich the Survival of the Fittest?"

Key Points: Questions:

Controversy and Debate

"The Welfare Dilemma"

Key Points: Questions:

Seeing Ourselves--National Map 7-1

"Median Household Income across the United States"

Key Points: Questions:

Window on the World--Global Map 7-1

"Income Disparity in Global Perspective"

Key Points: Questions:

8 Global Stratification

PART I: CHAPTER OUTLINE

I. Global Inequality: An Overview
    A.   A Word About Terminology
    B.   High-Income Countries
    C.   Middle-Income Countries
    D.   Low-Income Countries
II. Global Wealth and Poverty
    A.   The Severity of Poverty
    B.   The Extent of Poverty
    C.   Poverty and Children
    D.   Poverty and Women
    E.   Slavery
    F.   Correlates of Global Poverty
III. Global Inequality: Theoretical Analysis
    A.   Modernization Theory
    B.   Dependency Theory
IV. Global Inequality: Looking Ahead
V. Summary
VI. Key Concepts
VII. Critical-Thinking Questions
VIII. Learning Exercises

PART II: LEARNING OBJECTIVES

1. To be able to define and describe the demographics of the three "economic development" categories used to classify nations of the world.
2. To begin to understand both the severity and extensiveness of poverty in the low-income nations of the world.
3. To recognize the extent to which women are overrepresented among the poor of the world and the factors leading to this condition.
4. To be able to identify and discuss the correlates of global poverty.
5. To be able to identify and discuss the two major theories used to explain global inequality.
6. To be able to identify and describe the stages of modernization.

7. To be able to recognize the problems facing women as a result of modernization in the low-income nations of the world.
8. To be able to identify the keys to combating global inequality over the next century.

PART III: KEY CONCEPTS

absolute poverty
colonialism
dependency theory
high-income countries
low-income countries
middle-income countries
modernization theory
multinational corporation
neocolonialism
relative poverty
traditionalism

PART IV: IMPORTANT RESEARCHERS

Immanuel Wallerstein   W. W. Rostow

PART V: STUDY QUESTIONS

True-False

1.	T	F	The *high-income countries*, representing 15 percent of humanity, control over one-half of the world's income.
2.	T	F	Approximately 50 percent of the world's population live in *low-income countries*.
3.	T	F	Approximately one-fourth of the population of *low-income countries* live in urban areas.
4.	T	F	*Low-income countries* are plagued by constant hunger, unsafe housing, and high rates of disease.
5.	T	F	Only about 20 percent of the people living in *low-income societies* farm the land.
6.	T	F	*High-income countries* are by far the most advantaged economically, with 55 percent of the world's income supporting just 15 percent of the world's population.
7.	T	F	*Australia* has the highest quality of life score in the world.
8.	T	F	The death toll stemming from poverty is ten times greater than that resulting from all the world's armed conflicts.
9.	T	F	*Absolute poverty* refers to a lack of resources that is life threatening.

10.	T	F	*Gender inequality* is strongest in low-income societies.
11.	T	F	*Modernization theory* suggests the greatest barrier to economic development is *traditionalism*.
12.	T	F	*Modernization theory* draws criticism for suggesting that the causes of global poverty lie almost entirely in poor societies themselves.
13.	T	F	*Immanuel Wallerstein's* capitalist world economy model is used to illustrate and support *dependency theory*.
14.	T	F	*Dependency theory* claims that the increasing prosperity of high-income countries has largely come at the expense of low-income countries.
15.	T	F	According to *dependency theory*, global inequality must be seen in terms of the distribution of wealth, as opposed to highlighting the productivity of wealth.
16.	T	F	Ten million of the world's children die each year as a result of *hunger*.
17.	T	F	The keys to combating global inequality during the next century lie in seeing it as partly a *problem of technology* and also a *political problem*.
18.	T	F	As the low-income countries increase their standard of living, less stress is expected to be placed on the *physical environment*.

Multiple Choice

1. The poorest 20 percent of the world's nations controls _____ percent of the *global income*.

    (a) 12
    (b) 10
    (c) 15
    (d) 1
    (e) 5

2. The *high-income countries*, representing 15 percent of the world's population, control over _____ percent of the world's income.

    (a) 25
    (b) 35
    (c) 50
    (d) 80

3. *Middle-income countries* cover _____ percent of the earth's land area and contains one-third of humanity.

    (a) 10
    (b) 20
    (c) 30
    (d) 40
    (e) 50

4. What percentage of the world's population live in the *low-income countries* of the world?

(a) 50
(b) 60
(c) 77
(d) 85
(e) 95

5. The nickname of the Manila dump is:

(a) Rohooven Heights.
(b) Svendoven Mire.
(c) Swollen Hollow.
(d) Smokey Mountain.

6. The per-capita GDP in the United States is:

(a) $10,033.
(b) $51,300.
(c) $15,400.
(d) $26,997.
(e) $35,028.

7. Which country has the highest score on the *Quality of Life Index*?

(a) Canada
(b) the United States
(c) Brazil
(d) Germany

8. Half of all deaths in low-income countries occur among:

(a) the elderly beyond the age of 65.
(b) young adults 18-35.
(c) adults between the ages of 40 and 59.
(d) children under ten.

9. Which of the following is *not* a type of *slavery* identified in the text?

(a) chattel
(b) child
(c) debt bondage
(d) servile forms of marriage
(e) colonial

10. Which of the following is *not* discussed as a correlate of *global poverty*?

   (a) cultural patterns
   (b) population growth
   (c) technology
   (d) social stratification
   (e) all are discussed

11. A model of economic and social development that explains global inequality in terms of technological and cultural differences among societies is _____ theory.

   (a) colonial
   (b) dependency
   (c) modernization
   (d) ecological

12. *Neocolonialism* is:

   (a) primarily an overt political force.
   (b) a form of economic exploitation that does not involve formal political control.
   (c) the economic power of the low-income countries is being used to control the consumption patterns in the high-income countries.
   (d) the exploitation of the high-income countries by the low-income countries.
   (e) none of the above

13. *Modernization theory* identifies _____ as the greatest barrier to economic development.

   (a) technology
   (b) social equality
   (c) social power
   (d) tradition

14. Which of the following is *not* a stage in Rostow's model of modernization?

   (a) colonialism
   (b) traditional
   (c) take-off
   (d) drive to technological maturity
   (e) high mass consumption

15. According to *W. W. Rostow's* modernization model, which stage is Thailand currently in?

    (a)   traditional
    (b)   take-off
    (c)   drive to technological maturity
    (d)   high mass consumption
    (e)   residual-dependency

16. Which of the following is *not* a criticism of modernization theory?

    (a)   It tends to minimize the connection between rich and poor societies.
    (b)   It tends to blame the low-income countries for their own poverty.
    (c)   It ignores historical facts that thwart development in poor countries.
    (d)   It has fallen short of its own standards of success.
    (e)   all are criticisms of this theory

17. _____ *theory* is a model of economic and social development that explains global inequality in terms of the historical exploitation of poor societies by rich ones.

    (a)   Modernization
    (b)   Colonial
    (c)   Dependency
    (d)   Evolutionary
    (e)   Ecological

18. Which of the following is *not* mentioned in *Immanuel Wallerstein's* capitalist world-economy model as a reason for the perpetuation of the dependency of the low-income countries?

    (a)   narrow, export-oriented economies
    (b)   lack of industrial capacity
    (c)   foreign debt
    (d)   all are mentioned
    (e)   none are

19. Which of the following is *not* a criticism of dependency theory?

    (a)   It assumes that the wealth of the high-income countries is based solely on appropriating resources from low-income societies.
    (b)   It tends to blame the low-income countries for their own poverty.
    (c)   It does not lend itself to clear policy making.
    (d)   It assumes that world capitalism alone has produced global inequality.
    (e)   all of these are criticisms of this theory

20. In approximately _____ of the world's countries, living standards are lower than they were in 1980.

    (a)   one-third
    (b)   one-half
    (c)   three-fourths
    (d)   eighty-eight percent

Matching

1. ____ A model of economic and social development that explains global inequality in terms of the historical exploitation of poor societies by rich ones.
2. ____ The process by which some nations enrich themselves through political and economic control of other nations.
3. ____ The percentage of people in low-income countries who live in cities.
4. ____ Percentage of the world's income controlled by the poorest fifth of the world's population.
5. ____ Two high-income countries.
6. ____ The percentage of the world's population living in low-income countries.
7. ____ Huge businesses that operate in many countries.
8. ____ The percentage of births attended by trained health personnel in Mexico.
9. ____ A model of economic and social development that explains global inequality in terms of technological and cultural differences among societies.
10. ____ Two middle-income countries.

a.	Chile and Malaysia	f.	50
b.	modernization theory	g.	Canada and Singapore
c.	multinational corporations	h.	77
d.	colonialism	i.	dependency theory
e.	1	j.	25

Fill-In

1. Compared to the older "three worlds" model, the new classification system used in the text has two main advantages, including a focus on the single most important dimension that underlies social life-- _____ _____.

2. The *middle-income countries* of the world represent about _____ nations and _____ of the world's population.

3. According to our author, poverty in *low-income countries* is more _____ and more _____ than it is in the United States.

4. The United States had a GDP in 1995 of over _____ dollars.

5. The four types of slavery identified in the text include: _____, _____, _____ _____, and _____ forms of marriage.

6. The *correlates of global poverty* include _____, population _____, _____ patterns, social _____, _____ inequality, and global _____ relationships.

121

7. _____ is a new form of economic exploitation that does not involve formal political control.

8. _____ *theorists* suggest global inequality reflects differing levels of technological development and cultural differences among societies.

9. *W. W. Rostow's* stages of modernization, include: the _____, _____, drive to _____ maturity, and high mass _____.

10. _____ *theory* maintains that global poverty historically stems from the exploitation of poor societies by rich societies.

11. Immanuel Wallerstein calls the *rich nations* the _____ of the world economy. He refers to the *low-income* countries as the _____ of the world economy.

12. *Modernization theory* suggests that modern nations _____ _____ through technological innovation.

13. *Dependency theory* views global stratification in terms of how countries _____ _____.

14. In about _____ nations of the world, people are enjoying a higher *standard of living* than ever before. The overall pattern in the world however is toward *economic* _____ between the rich and poor nations.

15. Two key to combating global inequality during the next century will be seeing it partly as a problem of _____ and that it is also a _____ problem.

Definition and Short-Answer

1. Define the terms *high-income, middle-income,* and *low-income countries*. Identify the key characteristics of each category. Does this resolve the "terminology" problem?

2. How do the economies in each of the three *levels* or *categories* of countries differ from one another? Make specific reference to *Figures 11-1* and *11-2* in your answer.

3. What factors create the condition of *women* being overrepresented in poverty around the world?

4. What are the *correlates* of global poverty? Describe each.

5. What is *neocolonialism*? Provide an illustration.

6. What are the four stages of *modernization* in Rostow's model of societal change and development?

7. What are the *problems* faced by women in poor countries as a result of modernization?

8. According to *modernization* theorists, in what respects are rich nations part of the solution to global poverty?

9. Differentiate between how *modernization theory* and *dependency theory* view the primary causes of global inequality. Critique each of these theories, identifying the strengths and weaknesses of each in terms of explaining global poverty. How do each differ in terms of recommendations to improve the conditions in low-income countries.

10. Write an essay about *poverty in low-income countries*. What are the statistics of *global poverty*?

PART VI: ANSWERS TO STUDY QUESTIONS

True-False

1.	T	(p. 194)	10.	T	(p. 201)
2.	T	(p. 196)	11.	T	(p. 203)
3.	T	(p. 196)	12.	T	(p. 206)
4.	T	(p. 196)	13.	T	(p. 208)
5.	F	(p. 196)	14.	T	(p. 208)
6.	T	(p. 198)	15.	T	(pp. 209-210)
7.	T	(p. 199)	16.	T	(p. 213)
8.	T	(p. 199)	17.	T	(p. 214)
9.	T	(p. 199)	18.	F	(p. 214)

Multiple Choice

1.	d	(p. 194)	11.	c	(p. 203)
2.	c	(p. 195)	12.	b	(p. 203)
3.	d	(p. 196)	13.	d	(p. 205)
4.	a	(p. 196)	14.	a	(p. 205)
5.	b	(p. 197)	15.	b	(pp. 205-206)
6.	d	(p. 197)	16.	e	(pp. 206-207)
7.	a	(p. 198)	17.	c	(p. 208)
8.	d	(p. 200)	18.	d	(p. 209)
9.	e	(p. 201)	19.	b	(pp. 210-211)
10.	e	(pp. 201-203)	20.	a	(p. 212)

Matching

1.	i	(p. 208)	6.	f	(p. 196)
2.	d	(p. 203)	7.	c	(p. 203)
3.	j	(p. 196)	8.	h	(p. 201)
4.	e	(p. 194)	9.	b	(p. 203)
5.	g	(p. 195)	10.	a	(p. 196)

Fill-In

1. economic development (p. 194)
2. 90, one-third (p. 194)
3. severe, extensive (p. 197)
4. 6.9 trillion (p.. 198)
5. chattel, child, debt bondage, servile (p. 201)
6. technology, growth, cultural, stratification, gender, power (pp. 201-202)
7. neocolonialism (p. 203)
8. modernization (p. 203)

9. traditional, take-off, technological, consumption (pp. 205-206)
10. Dependency (p. 208)
11. core, periphery (p. 209)
12. produce wealth (p. 209)
13. distribute wealth (pp. 209-210)
14. 60, polarization (p. 212)
15. technology, political (p. 214)

PART VII: IN FOCUS—IMPORTANT ISSUES

• Define each of the following, proving three examples for each.

High-income countries:

Middle-income countries:

Low-income countries:

• The author of the text suggests that poverty in poor countries is *more severe* and *more extensive* than in rich countries. What evidence supports this statement?

Severe:

Extensive:

• Identify and illustrate the six *correlates of global poverty.*

• What is *modernization theory?*

What are the four stages in W.W. Rostow's theory of modernization?

According to modernization theory, what are the four roles played by rich nations in global economic development?

- What is *dependency theory*?

Immanuel Wallerstein's dependency theory involves what three factors?

According to dependency theory, what is the role of rich nations in world economic development?

PART VII: ANALYSIS AND COMMENT

Global Sociology

"Infanticide and Sexual Slavery: Reports from India and Thailand"

Key Points: Questions:

"A Different Kind of Poverty: A Report from India"

Key Points: Questions:

"Modernization and Women: A Report from Rural Bangladesh"

Key Points: Questions:

Controversy and Debate

"Will the World Starve?"

Key Points: Questions:

Window on the World--Global Maps 11-1 and 11-2

"Median Age at Death in Global Perspective"

Key Points: Questions:

"Prosperity and Stagnation in Global Perspective"

Key Points: Questions:

9 Sex and Gender

PART I: CHAPTER OUTLINE

PART II: LEARNING OBJECTIVES

1. To know the distinction between sex and gender.
2. To be able to distinguish between sex and sexual orientation.
3. To understand the cultural component in gender and sexual orientation.
4. To become aware of the various types of social organization based upon the relationship between females and males.
5. To be able to describe the link between patriarchy and sexism, and to see how the nature of each is changing in modern society.
6. To be able to describe the role that gender plays in socialization in the family, the peer group, schooling, the mass media, and adult interaction.
7. To see how gender stratification occurs in the work world, education, and politics.
8. To consider key arguments in the debate over whether women constitute a minority.
9. To consider how the structural-functional and social-conflict paradigms help explain the origins and persistence of gender inequality.
10. To begin to recognize the extent to which women are victims of violence, and to begin to understand what we can do to change this problem.
11. To consider the central ideas of feminism, the types of feminism and opposition to feminism.

PART III: KEY CONCEPTS

bisexual
expressive qualities
femininity
feminism
gender
gender identity
gender roles
gender stratification
heterosexuality
hermaphrodite
homophobia
homosexual
instrumental qualities
kibbutzim
liberal feminism
masculinity
matriarchy
patriarchy
pornography
radical feminism
sex

sexual harassment
sexual orientation
socialist feminism
transsexuals

PART IV: IMPORTANT RESEARCHERS

Alfred Kinsey   Margaret Mead

George Murdock   Talcott Parsons

Jesse Bernard   Janet Lever

Carol Gilligan   Friedrich Engels

PART V: STUDY QUESTIONS

True-False

1.	T	F	*Hermaphrodites* are scorned and viewed negatively in all known societies.
2.	T	F	The attraction to *neither sex* is referred to as *asexuality*.
3.	T	F	The research by *Alfred Kinsey* suggests sexual orientations may not be mutually exclusive.
4.	T	F	*Gender* refers to the biological distinction between females and males.
5.	T	F	The experience of the *Israeli Kibbutzim* suggests that cultures have considerable latitude in defining what is masculine and feminine.
6.	T	F	The conclusions made by *Margaret Mead* in her research on three New Guinea societies is consistent with the sociobiological argument that "persistent biological distinctions may undermine gender equality."

7.	T	F	*George Murdock's* cross-cultural research has shown some general patterns in terms of which type of activities are classified as *masculine* or *feminine,* however, beyond this general pattern, significant variation exists.
8.	T	F	In global perspective, societies consistently define only a few specific activities as *feminine* or *masculine.*
9.	T	F	*Patriarchy* is a form of social organization in which males dominate females.
10.	T	F	Research suggests that the vast majority of young people in the United States develop consistently "masculine" or "feminine" personalities.
11.	T	F	*Carol Gilligan's* research on patterns of moral reasoning suggests that boys learn to reason according to "rules and principles" more so than girls.
12.	T	F	In 1997, 59.8 percent of women in the U.S. aged sixteen and over were working for income. Three-fourths of these women did so full-time.
13.	T	F	Women with children under the age of six years have a much smaller proportion of their number working in the labor force than married women with no children.
14.	T	F	Approximately two-thirds of the *pay gap* between men and women is the result of two factors--types of work and family responsibilities.
15.	T	F	Women earn over fifty percent of the bachelor's degrees granted in the United States.
16.	T	F	*Minority females* earn more on average than minority males.
17.	T	F	According to the definition given in the text, *sexual harassment* always involves physical contact.
18.	T	F	According to structural-functionalist Talcott Parsons, gender, at least in the traditional sense, forms a *complementary* set of roles that links men and women together.
19.	T	F	The *ERA* was first proposed to Congress in 1972.
20.	T	F	The ideology of *liberal feminism* respects the family as a social institution.

Multiple Choice

1. _____ refers to the biological distinction between females and males.

    (a)   Sex
    (b)   Gender
    (c)   Sexuality
    (d)   Sexual orientation

2. The female embryo will develop if:

    (a)   the father contributes an X chromosome and the mother contributes an X chromosome.
    (b)   the father contributes an X chromosome and the mother contributes a Y chromosome.
    (c)   the mother contributes an X chromosome and the father contributes a Y chromosome.
    (d)   the mother contributes a Y chromosome and the father contributes a Y chromosome.

3. A hormone imbalance before birth that results in the birth of a child with some combination of male and female internal and external genitals is termed a(n):

   (a) transsexual.
   (b) bisexual.
   (c) hermaphrodite.
   (d) aphrodisiac.

4. What is the term for an individual's preference in terms of sexual partners?

   (a) sexuality
   (b) sexual experience
   (c) sexual identity
   (d) sexual orientation

5. Alfred Kinsey describes *sexual orientation* as a:

   (a) dichotomy.
   (b) continuum.
   (c) myth.
   (d) tool used by the powerful to exploit the masses.

6. Investigations of the *Israeli Kibbutzim* have indicated:

   (a) they are collective settlements.
   (b) their members historically have embraced social equality.
   (c) they support evidence of wide cultural latitude in defining what is feminine and masculine.
   (d) men and women living there share both work and decision making.
   (e) all of the above

7. The social inequality of men and women has been shown to be culturally based rather than exclusively biological by which of the following studies:

   (a) Murdock's study of preindustrial societies
   (b) Israeli kibbutzim studies
   (c) New Guinea studies by Margaret Mead
   (d) all of the above

8. Margaret Mead's research on gender in three societies in New Guinea illustrates that:

   (a) diffusion tends to standardize gender role assignments for women and men.
   (b) gender is primarily biologically determined.
   (c) gender is treated virtually the same across societies.
   (d) gender is a variable creation of culture.
   (e) while gender roles vary cross-culturally for men, they are very consistent for women

9. Among the *Mundugumor*, Margaret Mead found:

   (a)   both females and males to be very passive.
   (b)   females to be very aggressive and males to be passive.
   (c)   both males and females to be aggressive and hostile.
   (d)   sex roles to be very similar to what they are in the U.S.

10. A form of social organization in which females are dominated by males is termed:

    (a)   matriarchal.
    (b)   oligarchal.
    (c)   patriarchy.
    (d)   egalitarian.

11. Which sociologist suggests that, soon after birth, family members introduce infants to either a *pink* or a *blue* world, depending on whether the infant is a she or a he?

    (a)   Karl Marx
    (b)   Jesse Bernard
    (c)   George Peter Murdock
    (d)   Talcott Parsons

12. Research by Carol Gilligan and Janet Lever demonstrates the influence of _____ on gender roles.

    (a)   the peer group
    (b)   biology
    (c)   religion
    (d)   personality

13. Which of the following statements about women in the labor force is *inaccurate*?

    (a)   Most married women are in the paid labor force.
    (b)   Most married women without children are in the paid labor force.
    (c)   Most married women with children under the age of six are in the paid labor force.
    (d)   About 46 percent of all women in the paid labor force work in either clerical or service type jobs.
    (e)   Less than one-half of all divorced women with children work in the paid labor force.

14. On average, what percentage of a male's income does a female earn?

    (a)   39
    (b)   48
    (c)   57
    (d)   74
    (e)   89

15. After the 1998 national elections, how many of the 100 U.S. Senators were women?

    (a)   none
    (b)   2
    (c)   9
    (d)   20

16. As a woman, where are you most likely to suffer *physical violence*?

    (a)   at work
    (b)   at home
    (c)   among friends
    (d)   on the streets

17. *Talcott Parsons* argued that there exist two *complementary role sets* which link males and females together with social institutions. He called these:

    (a)   rational and irrational.
    (b)   effective and affective.
    (c)   fundamental and secondary.
    (d)   residual and basic.
    (e)   instrumental and expressive.

18. Which theorist suggested that the male dominance over women was linked to technological advances which led to surpluses of valued resources?

    (a)   Talcott Parsons
    (b)   Erving Goffman
    (c)   Friedrich Engels
    (d)   Janet Lever

19. Which of the following nations has the highest rate of *contraception use* by married women of childbearing age?

    (a)   Norway
    (b)   Uganda
    (c)   the United States
    (d)   Ireland

20. Which of the following is *not* a variation with *feminism*?

    (a)   liberal
    (b)   socialist
    (c)   radical
    (d)   expressive

Matching

1. ____ The biological distinction between females and males.
2. ____ An individual's preference in terms of sexual partners.
3. ____ The significance society attaches to the biological categories of females and male.
4. ____ The advocacy of social equality for the men and women in opposition to patriarchy and sexism.
5. ____ The belief that one sex is innately superior to the other.
6. ____ The father's chromosome that results in a male embryo.
7. ____ A society's unequal distribution of wealth, power, and privilege between men and women.
8. ____ The chromosome always contributed by the mother.
9. ____ Attitudes and activities that a society links to each sex.
10. ____ A human being with some combination of female and male genitalia.
11. ____ Did cross-cultural research on gender roles and suggested culture largely determined differences in the relative statuses and roles of females and males.
12. ____ A structural-functionalist, differentiated between instrumental and expressive roles.
13. ____ Believed technological advancement led to a production surplus and greater *social inequality*.
14. ____ A form of social organization in which *males dominate females*.

a.	sexual orientation	h.	sex
b.	feminism	i.	hermaphrodite
c.	Margaret Mead	j.	gender roles
d.	gender	k.	Talcott Parsons
e.	gender stratification	l.	X chromosome
f.	patriarchy	m.	Freidrich Engels
g.	Y chromosome	n.	sexism

Fill-In

1. _____ refers to the biological distinction between females and males.
2. *Sexual* _____ is an individual's preference in terms of sexual partners.
3. The irrational fear of gay people is known as _____.
4. _____ refers to the significance a society attaches to biological categories of female and male.
5. According to research cited in the text, adolescent males exhibit greater _____ ability, while adolescent females excel in _____ skills.
6. In her research on gender roles, Margaret Mead focused on three New Guinea societies, the _____, _____, and the _____.
7. In George Murdock's study of more than 200 preindustrial societies, he found some global agreement on which tasks are *feminine* and which, *masculine*. _____ and _____, Murdock observed, generally fall to men, while _____ tasks tend to be women's work. With their simple technology, preindustrial societies apparently assign roles reflecting men's and women's _____ attributes. Beyond this general pattern, Murdock found significant _____.
8. _____ is a form of social organization in which *females dominate males*.

9.   According to Jessie Bernard, infants are brought home to two different worlds, the _____, and the _____.

10.   Research by Janet Lever has found that games typically played by girls has few _____ and rarely is _____ a goal.

11.   *Gender* _____ refers to a society's unequal distribution of wealth, power, and privilege between men and women.

12.   The *beauty myth* arises because society teaches women to measure themselves in terms of _____ _____, and is also derived from the way society teaches women to prize _____ with _____.

13.   In the United States, _____ percent of women over the age of 16 were working for income in 1997. The comparable figure for men was _____.

14.   Almost one-half of all working women fall within two broad *occupational categories*: _____ and _____.

15.   In 1994, for every dollar earned by men, women earned _____.

16.   Women were barred from voting in the U.S. until passage of the _____ Amendment to the Constitution in _____.

17.   The two types of *violence* against women focused on in the text include _____ and _____.

18.   Talcott Parsons identified two *complementary roles* that link men and women. These include the _____ and _____.

19.   Basic *feminist ideas* include the importance of _____, the expanding human _____, eliminating gender _____, ending sexual _____, and promoting sexual _____.

20.   The three types of *feminism* are _____, _____, and _____.

Definition and Short-Answer

1.   Briefly review the significant events in the history of the *Women's Movement* during the nineteenth century.

2.   What does *Alfred Kinsey* mean by the statement that "in many cases, sexual orientations are not mutually exclusive?"

3.   Compare the research by *Margaret Mead* in New Guinea with the research done at the Israeli *Kibbutzim* in terms of the cultural variability of gender roles.

4.   What generalizations about the linkage between *sex* and *gender* can be made based on the cross-cultural research of *George Murdock*?

5.   According to the author, is *patriarchy* inevitable? Why? What roles have technological advances and industrialization played in the changes in the relative statuses of women and men in society?

6.   *Table 9-1* presents lists of traits linked to the traditional gender identities of *femininity* and *masculinity*. Develop a questionnaire using the traits identified in this table to survey females and males to determine to what extent these traits differentiate between the sexes.

7.   Identify five important points about *gender stratification* within the occupational domain of our society.

8.   What are the explanations as to why males dominate *politics*? To what extent are the roles of women changing in this sphere of social life? What factors are influencing these changes?

9.   Review the issue of *violence against women* in our society. What are the types of violence discussed? What are the demographics of violence?

10. Are women a *minority group*? What are the arguments for and against this idea?
11. Compare the analyses of gender stratification as provided through the *structural-functional* and *social-conflict* paradigms.
12. What are the five *basic principles* of *feminism*? Discuss the specific examples for each.
13. What are the three types of *feminism*? Briefly differentiate between them in terms of the basic arguments being made about gender roles in society.
14. What are the three general criticisms of the conclusions being made by *social-conflict* theorists concerning gender stratification?
15. What evidence can you provide from your own experience and observations concerning the argument being made by *Jesse Bernard* about the *pink* and *blue* worlds?

PART VI: ANSWERS TO STUDY QUESTIONS

True-False

1.	F	(p. 220)	11.	T	(p. 226)
2.	T	(p. 220)	12.	T	(p. 227)
3.	T	(p. 221)	13.	F	(p. 229)
4.	F	(p. 222)	14.	T	(p. 230)
5.	T	(p. 222)	15.	T	(p. 231)
6.	F	(p. 222)	16.	F	(p. 233)
7.	T	(p. 223)	17.	F	(p. 234)
8.	F	(p. 223)	18.	T	(p. 236)
9.	T	(p. 223)	19.	F	(p. 238)
10.	F	(p. 225)	20.	T	(p. 239)

Multiple-Choice

1.	a	(p. 219)	11.	b	(p. 225)
2.	c	(p. 219)	12.	a	(p. 226)
3.	c	(p. 220)	13.	e	(pp. 227-229)
4.	d	(p. 220)	14	d	(p. 230)
5.	b	(p. 221)	15.	c	(p. 232)
6.	e	(p. 222)	16.	b	(p. 234)
7.	d	(pp. 222-223)	17.	e	(p. 236)
8.	d	(pp. 222-223)	18.	c	(p. 237)
9.	b	(p. 223)	19.	a	(p. 239)
10.	c	(p. 223)	20.	d	(p. 239)

Matching

1.	h	(p. 219)	8.	l	(p. 219)
2.	a	(p. 220)	9.	j	(p. 225)
3.	d	(p. 222)	10.	i	(p. 220)
4.	b	(p. 237)	11.	c	(p. 222)

5.	n	(p. 224)	12.	k	(p. 236)
6.	g	(p. 219)	13.	m	(p. 237)
7.	e	(p. 227)	14.	f	(p. 223)

Fill-In

1. Sex (p. 219)
2. orientation (p. 220)
3. homophobia (p. 221)
4. Gender (p. 222)
5. mathematical, verbal (p. 222)
6. Arapesh, Mundugamor, Tchambuli (pp. 222-223)
7. warfare, hunting, home-centered, physical, variation (p. 223)
8. Matriarchy (p. 322)
9. pink, blue (p. 225)
10. rules, victory (p. 226)
11. stratification (p. 227)
12. physical appearance, relationships, men (p. 326)
13. 59.8, 74.9 (p. 227)
14. administrative support, service (p. 229)
15. 74 cents (p. 230)
16. nineteenth, 1920 (p. 231)
17. sexual harassment, pornography (pp. 234-235)
18. instrumental, expressive (p. 236)
19. change, choice, stratification, violence, autonomy (p. 238)
20. liberal, socialist, radical (pp. 238-239)

PART VII: IN FOCUS-IMPORTANT ISSUES

- Summarize the findings and conclusions about *gender* by the following researchers/research:

Margaret Mead:

George Murdock:

Israeli kibbutzim:

- Review one major point made in the text about *gender and socialization* for each of the following areas:

  Family:

  Peer Group:

  Schooling:

- Provide three examples of *gender stratification* in our society:

- In a paragraph, summarize the major arguments being made for each of the following theories concerning gender role patterns around the world.

  Structural-Functionalism:

    Critical evaluation:

  Social-Conflict:

    Critical evaluation:

- What are the five general principles of *feminism?*

- Describe each of the following three *types of feminism*.

  Liberal:

  Socialist:

  Radical:

PART VIII: ANALYSIS AND COMMENT

Critical Thinking

"Pretty Is as Pretty Does: The Beauty Myth"

Key Points: Questions:

Exploring Cyber-Society

"Pornography: As Close as Your Computer"

Key Points: Questions:

Controversy and Debate

"Men's Rights! Are Men Really So Privileged?"

Key Points: Questions:

Window on the World--Global Map 9-1 and 9-2

"Women's Power in Global Perspective"

Key Points: Questions:

"Women's Paid Employment in Global Perspective"

Key Points: Questions:

Seeing Ourselves--National Map 9-1

"Women in State Government across the U.S."

Key Points: Questions:

10 Race and Ethnicity

PART I: CHAPTER OUTLINE

PART II: LEARNING OBJECTIVES

1. To develop an understanding about the biological basis for definitions of race.
2. To be able to distinguish between the biological concept of race and the cultural concept of ethnicity.
3. To be able to identify the characteristics of a minority group.
4. To be able to identify and describe the two forms of prejudice.
5. To be able to identify and describe the four theories of prejudice.
6. Be able to distinguish between prejudice and discrimination.
7. To be able to provide examples of institutional prejudice and discrimination.

8.   To be able to see how prejudice and discrimination combine to create a vicious cycle.
9.   To be able to describe the patterns of interaction between minorities and the majority.
10.   To be able to describe the histories and relative statuses of each of the racial and ethnic groups identified in the text.
11.   To consider the advantages and disadvantages of affirmative action policies in our society.
12.   To analyze the projections about demographic patterns for the next century concerning race and ethnicity.

PART III: KEY CONCEPTS

affirmative action
American dilemma
assimilation
authoritarian personality
Brown vs. the Board of Education of Topeka
de facto segregation
de jure segregation
discrimination
ethnicity
genocide
hypersegregation
institutional discrimination
institutional prejudice
minority
miscegenation
pluralism
prejudice
race
racism
scapegoat theory
segregation
stereotype
WASP
white ethnics

PART IV: IMPORTANT RESEARCHERS

Robert Merton   Emory Bogardus

T. W. Adorno   Thomas Sowell

PART V: STUDY QUESTIONS

True-False

1.   T   F   According to the author of our text, for sociological purposes the concepts of *race* and *ethnicity* can be used interchangeably.

2.   T   F   *Ethnicity* is defined as a category of men and women who share biologically transmitted traits that members of society deem socially important.

3.   T   F   A racial or ethnic *minority* is a category of people, distinguished by physical or cultural traits, who are socially disadvantaged.

4.   T   F   According to the author, *ethnicity* involves even more variability and mixture than *race* does, for most people identify with more than one ethnic background.

5.   T   F   The *scapegoat theory* links prejudice to frustration and suggests that prejudice is likely to be pronounced among people who themselves are disadvantaged.

6.   T   F   Emory Bogardus' concept of *social distance* is used in the *cultural theory* of prejudice, which suggests that some prejudice is found in everyone because it is embedded in culture.

7.   T   F   In *Robert Merton's* typology of patterns of prejudice and discrimination an unprejudiced-nondiscriminator is labeled an "all-weather liberal."

8.   T   F   According to the author, as a cultural process, *assimilation* involves changes in ethnicity but not in race.

9.   T   F   Supreme Court decisions such as the *1954 Brown case* have reduced the presence of *de jure discrimination* in the United States.

10.   T   F   *Genocide* is the systematic annihilation of one category of people by another.

11.   T   F   *Native Americans* were not granted citizenship in the United States until 1924.

12.   T   F   The *Dred Scott* Supreme Court decision declared that blacks were to have full rights and privileges as citizens of the United States.

13.   T   F   *Jim Crow Laws* illustrate institutional discrimination.

14.   T   F   The largest category of *Asian Americans* is people of Chinese ancestry.

15.   T   F   Though a "silent minority," *Chinese Americans* have higher poverty rates and lower average family incomes than African Americans and Hispanics.

16.   T   F   *Issei* is a term referring to foreign-born Japanese.

17.   T   F   More than one-half of *Hispanics* in the United States are *Mexican Americans*.

18.   T   F   *Cuban Americans* have the lowest average family income and highest poverty rates of all Hispanic Americans.

19.   T   F   The highest rates of *immigration* to the United States occurred during the 1920s and 1930s.

20.   T   F   Two major criticisms of *affirmative action* is that it polarizes people and that it benefits those people who need it least.

1. Linda Brown was not permitted to enroll in the second grade at an elementary school near her home in Topeka, Kansas because she was:

    (a)   Jewish.
    (b)   African American.
    (c)   blind.
    (d)   HIV positive.
    (e)   Iranian.

2. A category of men and women who share biologically transmitted traits that members of a society deem socially significant, is the definition for:

    (a)   race.
    (b)   minority group.
    (c)   ethnicity.
    (d)   assimilation.

3. Today in the United States, *interracial births* account for _____ percent of all births.

    (a)   less than 1
    (b)   2
    (c)   4
    (d)   6
    (e)   9

4. A shared cultural heritage is the definition for:

    (a)   a minority group.
    (b)   race.
    (c)   assimilation.
    (d)   pluralism.
    (e)   ethnicity.

5. Members of an ethnic category share:

    (a)   common ancestors, language, and religion.
    (b)   only biological distinctions.
    (c)   residential location.
    (d)   social class ranking.

6. Among people of *European descent,* the largest number of people in the U.S. trace their ancestry back to:

    (a) Italy.
    (b) Ireland.
    (c) England.
    (d) Germany.
    (e) Russia.

7. *Minority groups* have two major characteristics:

    (a) race and ethnicity
    (b) religion and ethnicity
    (c) physical traits and political orientation
    (d) sexual orientation and race
    (e) distinctive identity and subordination

8. What is the terms for a category of people, set apart by physical or cultural traits, that is socially disadvantaged?

    (a) minority group
    (b) stereotype
    (c) ethnicity
    (d) race

9. What is the term for a rigid and irrational generalization about an entire category of people?

    (a) racism
    (b) discrimination
    (c) stereotype
    (d) prejudice

10. What is the term for biased characterizations of some category of people?

    (a) racism
    (b) stereotype
    (c) discrimination
    (d) prejudice

11. A *form of prejudice* that views certain categories of people as innately inferior is called:

    (a) stereotyping.
    (b) discrimination.
    (c) racism.
    (d) scapegoating.

12. One explanation of the origin of prejudice is found in the concept of the *authoritarian personality*. Such a personality exhibits:

    (a) an attitude of authority over others believed to be inferior.
    (b) frustration over personal troubles directed toward someone less powerful.
    (c) rigid conformity to cultural norms and values.
    (d) social distance from others deemed inferior.

13. *Robert Merton's* study of the relationship between prejudice and discrimination revealed one behavioral type that discriminates against persons even though he or she is not prejudiced. This person would be called a(n):

    (a) active bigot.
    (b) all-weather liberal.
    (c) timid bigot.
    (d) fair-weather liberal.

14. According to the work of W. I. Thomas, a *vicious cycle* is formed by which variables?

    (a) miscegenation and authoritarianism
    (b) race and ethnicity
    (c) pluralism and assimilation
    (d) segregation and integration
    (e) prejudice and discrimination

15. *Prejudice* refers to attitudes, and discrimination involves:

    (a) adopting patterns of the dominant culture.
    (b) beliefs and emotions.
    (c) oversimplified generalizations.
    (d) treating various categories of people unequally.

16. A state in which people of all races and ethnicities are distinct, but have social parity is termed:

    (a) segregation.
    (b) pluralism.
    (c) integration.
    (d) assimilation.

17. *Pluralism* has only limited application in U.S. society because:

    (a) most Americans only want to maintain their distinctive identities to a point.
    (b) our society's tolerance for diversity is limited.
    (c) people of different colors and cultures don't have equal standing.
    (d) all of the above

18. *Miscegenation* is:

    (a)   the biological reproduction by partners of different racial categories.
    (b)   the process by which minorities gradually adopt patterns of the dominant culture.
    (c)   a state in which all categories of people are distinct but have social parity.
    (d)   a condition of prejudice leading to discrimination.

19. In _____ the U.S. government made Native Americans wards of the state and set out to resolve the "Indian problem."

    (a)   1770
    (b)   1807
    (c)   1871
    (d)   1911
    (e)   1946

20. *Jim Crow Laws:*

    (a)   protected freed slaves prior to the Civil War.
    (b)   gave Native Americans residency rights west of the Mississippi.
    (c)   integrated schools.
    (d)   are examples of institutional discrimination.
    (e)   emerged during the post-World War II economic boom period.

21. Approximately what percentage of African Americans are living in poverty today?

    (a)   10
    (b)   41
    (c)   19
    (d)   62
    (e)   24

22. Which category of *Asian Americans* has the highest median family income?

    (a)   Chinese
    (b)   Filipino
    (c)   Japanese
    (d)   Korean

23. *Mexican Americans* account for _____ of all Hispanics living in the United States.

    (a)   one-third
    (b)   two-thirds
    (c)   one-fifth
    (d)   one-half

147

24. Today, most immigrants to the U.S. come from:

    (a)   Latin America and Asia.
    (b)   India and Europe.
    (c)   Europe and Africa.
    (d)   Africa and India.
    (e)   The Middle East and Europe.

Matching

1. ____ A category of men and women who share biologically transmitted traits that members of a society deem socially significant.
2. ____ An approach contending that while extreme prejudice may characterize some people, some prejudice is found in everyone.
3. ____ Hostility toward foreigners.
4. ____ A person or category of people, typically with little power, whom people unfairly blame for their troubles.
5. ____ A theory holding that prejudice springs from frustration among people who are themselves disadvantaged.
6. ____ The process by which minorities gradually adopt patterns of the dominant culture.
7. ____ A state in which all races and ethnicities while distinct, have social parity.
8. ____ A shared cultural heritage.
9. ____ Non-WASPs whose ancestors lived in Ireland, Poland, Germany, Italy, or other European countries.
10. ____ A category of people, distinguished by physical or cultural traits, that is socially disadvantaged.

a.	xenophobia	f.	white ethnic Americans
b.	assimilation	g.	cultural theory
c.	minority	h.	pluralism
d.	scapegoat	i.	race
e.	ethnicity	j.	scapegoat theory

Fill-In

1. In 1954, the Supreme Court of the United States ruled unanimously that _____ segregated schools inevitably provide _____ _____ with inferior schooling, thus striking down a ruling, dating back to 1896, that permitted "separate but equal" education.
2. The term _____ refers to a category composed of men and women who share biologically transmitted traits that members of society deem socially significant.
3. The three part scheme of racial classification developed by biologists during the nineteenth century included _____, _____, and _____. Sociologists consider such terms misleading at best, since we know that no society contains biologically "pure" people.
4. While *race* is a _____ concept, *ethnicity* is a _____ concept.

5. Two major characteristics of *minorities* are that they have a _____ identity and are _____ by the social-stratification system.

6. A _____ refers to biased categorizations of some category of people.

7. _____ *theory* holds that prejudice springs from frustration.

8. Thomas Sowell has demonstrated that most of the documented racial difference in intelligence are not due to _____ but to people's _____.

9. _____ prejudice and discrimination refers to bias in attitudes or actions inherent in the operation of any of society's institutions.

10. _____ is the process by which minorities gradually adopt patterns of the dominant culture.

11. _____ is the systematic annihilation of one category of people by another.

12. In _____, the United States declared Native Americans wards of the government and set out to resolve "the Indian problem" through forced assimilation. Not until _____ were Native Americans entitled to U.S. citizenship.

13. In the _____ _____ *case* of 1857, the U.S. Supreme Court addressed the question, "Are blacks citizens?" by writing "We think they are not...."

14. *Gunnar Myrdal* argued that the denial of basic rights and freedoms to entire categories of Americans was the _____.

15. In 1865, the _____ Amendment to the Constitution outlawed slavery.

16. In 1997 the *median family income* for the entire population of the U.S. was $42,300. For *African Americans* this figure was _____.

17. In 1998, *Hispanics* represented _____ percent of the U.S. population.

18. More than _____ *immigrants* have come to the U.S. each year during the 1990s.

Short-Answer and Definition

1. Identify and describe the four *explanations* of why prejudice exists.
2. Differentiate between the concepts *prejudice* and *discrimination*.
3. What are the four types of people identified by *Robert Merton's* typology of patterns of prejudice and discrimination? Provide an illustration for each.
4. What is *institutional prejudice and discrimination*? Provide two illustrations.
5. What are three criticisms of *affirmative action*? What are three reasons given by proponents of affirmative action to continue this social policy.
6. What are the four models representing the *patterns of interaction* between minority groups and the majority group? Define and discuss an illustration for each of these.
7. In what three important ways did Japanese immigration and assimilation into U.S. society differ from the Chinese?
8. How do Native Americans, African Americans, Hispanic Americans, and Asian Americans compare to whites in terms of relative social standing using the variables of *educational achievement, family income,* and *poverty rates.*
9. What was the *Dred Scott* ruling by the Supreme Court?
10. What was the Court's ruling in *Brown versus the Board of Education of Topeka case*?

11. What is the *American Dilemma*?
12. What does scientific research reveal about the relationship between race and *intelligence*?
13. What are the two major characteristics of a *minority group*?
14. Differentiate between the concepts of *race* and *ethnicity*.
15. How are the changing patterns in *immigration* likely to influence the future of the United States?

PART VI: ANSWERS TO STUDY QUESTIONS

True-False

1.	F	(p. 245)	11.	T	(p. 256)
2.	F	(p. 247)	12.	F	(p. 258)
3.	T	(p. 248)	13.	T	(p. 259)
4.	T	(p. 248)	14.	T	(pp. 259-260)
5.	T	(p. 250)	15.	F	(p. 260)
6.	T	(p. 251)	16.	T	(p. 261)
7.	T	(p. 252)	17.	T	(p. 264)
8.	T	(p. 254)	18.	F	(p. 264)
9.	T	(p. 254)	19.	F	(p. 267)
10.	T	(p. 254)	20.	T	(p. 267)

Multiple Choice

1.	b	(p. 245)	13.	d	(p. 252)
2.	a	(p. 246)	14.	e	(p. 252)
3.	c	(p. 247)	15.	d	(p. 252)
4.	e	(p. 247)	16.	b	(p. 253)
5.	a	(p. 247)	17.	d	(p. 253)
6.	d	(p. 247)	18.	a	(p. 254)
7.	e	(p. 248)	19.	c	(p. 256)
8.	a	(p. 248)	20.	d	(p. 259)
9.	d	(p. 249)	21.	e	(p. 259)
10.	b	(p. 249)	22.	c	(p. 260)
11.	c	(p. 249)	23.	b	(p. 264)
12.	c	(p. 251)	24.	a	(p. 267)

Matching

1.	i	(p. 246)	6.	b	(p. 253)
2.	g	(p. 251)	7.	h	(p. 253)
3.	a	(p. 267)	8.	e	(p. 247)
4.	d	(p. 250)	9.	f	(p. 265)
5.	j	(p. 250)	10.	c	(p. 248)

1. racial, African American (p. 245)
2. race (p. 246)
3. Caucasian, Negroid, Mongoloid (p. 246)
4. biological, cultural (p. 247)
5. distinctive, subordination (p. 248)
6. stereotype (p. 249)
7. Scapegoat (p. 250)
8. biology, environments (p. 251)
9. Institutional (p. 252)
10. assimilation (p. 253)
11. Genocide (p. 254)
12. 1871, 1924 (p. 256)
13. Dred Scott (p. 258)
14. American dilemma (p. 258)
15. Thirteenth (p. 258)
16. $28,602 (p. 259)
17. 11 (p. 264)
18. 1 million (p. 267)

PART VII: IN FOCUS: MAJOR IDEAS

*   Define the terms *race* and *ethnicity*:

*   Differentiate between *prejudice* and *discrimination*:

- Define and illustrate the following *theories of prejudice*:

  Scapegoat theory   Authoritarian Personality theory

  Cultural theory   Conflict theory

- Define and illustrate the following *patterns of interaction* between majority and minority groups:

  Pluralism   Assimilation

  Segregation   Genocide

- What are the major characteristics of a *minority group*?

- Identify three important points being made about the following racial and ethnic categories in the United States:

  Native Americans   White Anglo-Saxon Protestants

African Americans   Asian Americans

Hispanic Americans   White Ethnic Americans

PART VIII: ANALYSIS AND COMMENT

Critical Thinking

"Does Race Affect Intelligence?"

Key Points: Questions:

Controversy and Debate

"Affirmative Action: Problem or Solution?"

Key Points: Questions:

Seeing Ourselves--National Maps 10-1, 10-2, 10-3

"Where the Minority-Majority Already Exists"

Key Points: Questions:

"The Concentration of People of WASP Ancestry across the United States"

Key Points: Questions:

"The Concentration of Hispanics/Latinos, African Americans, and Asian Americans, by County, Projections for 2001"

Key Points: Questions:

11 Economics and Politics

PART I: CHAPTER OUTLINE

I. The Economy: Historical Overview
    A. The Agricultural Revolution
    B. The Industrial Revolution
    C. The Information Revolution and the Postindustrial Society
    D. Sectors of the Economy
    E. The Global Economy
II. Economic Systems: Paths to Justice
    A. Capitalism
    B. Socialism
    C. Welfare Capitalism and State Capitalism
    D. Relative Advantages of Capitalism and Socialism
    E. Changes in Socialist Countries
III. Work in the Postindustrial Economy
    A. The Changing Workplace
    B. Labor Unions
    C. Professions
    D. Self-Employment
    E. Unemployment
    F. Social Diversity in the Work Place
    G. New Information Technology and Work
IV. Corporations
    A. Economic Concentration
    B. Corporate Linkages
    C. Corporations: Are they Competitive?
    D. Corporations and the Global Economy
V. Looking Ahead: The Economy of the Twenty-First Century
VI. Politics: Historical Overview
VII. Global Political Systems
    A. Monarchy
    B. Democracy
    C. Authoritarianism
    D. Totalitarianism
    E. A Global Political System?

PART II: LEARNING OBJECTIVES

1.   To be able to identify the elements of the economy.
2.   To be able to review the history and development of economic activity from the Agricultural Revolution through to the Postindustrial Revolution.
3.   To be able to identify and describe the three sectors of the economy.
4.   To be able to compare the economic systems of capitalism, state capitalism, socialism, and democratic socialism.
5.   To be able to explain the difference between socialism and communism.
6.   To be able to describe the general characteristics and trends of work in the U.S. postindustrial society.
7.   To begin to see the impact of multinational corporations on the world economy.
8.   To recognize the difference between power and authority.
9.   To be able to identify, define, and illustrate the different types of authority.
10.   To be able to compare the four principal kinds of political systems.
11.   To be able to describe the nature of the American political system of government, and discuss the principal characteristics of the political spectrum of the U.S.

12. To be able to compare the pluralist and power-elite models of political power.
13. To be able to describe the types of political power that exceed, or seek to eradicate, established politics.
14. To be able to identify the factors which increase the likelihood of war.
15. To recognize the historical pattern of militarism in the United States and around the world, and to consider factors which can be used in the pursuit of peace.

PART III: KEY CONCEPTS

Economics:

capitalism
communism
conglomerates
corporation
economy
interlocking directorate
labor unions
monopoly
oligopoly
postindustrial economy
primary sector
profession
secondary sector
socialism
state capitalism
tertiary sector
welfare capitalism

Politics:

arms race
authoritarianism
authority
charismatic authority
democracy
government
Marxist political-economy model
military-industrial complex
monarchy
pluralist model
Political Action Committees
politics
power
power-elite model

rational-legal authority
revolution
routinization of charisma
special-interest group
state terrorism
totalitarianism
traditional authority
voter apathy
war

PART IV: IMPORTANT RESEARCHERS

Karl Marx   Max Weber

C. Wright Mills   Robert and Helen Lynd

Quincy Wright   Floyd Hunter

Robert Dahl   Nelson Polsby

PART V: STUDY QUESTIONS

True-False--Economics

1. T   F   The *economy* includes the production, distribution, and consumption of both goods and services.
2. T   F   *Agriculture*, as a subsistence strategy, first emerged some five thousand years ago.
3. T   F   The *primary sector* of the economy is the part of the economy that generates raw material directly from the natural environment.
4. T   F   The terms *primary, secondary,* and *tertiary* referring to sectors in the economy, imply a ranking in importance for our society.
5. T   F   *Socialism* is being defined as both a political and economic system.
6. T   F   Per capita GDP tended to be significantly higher in capitalist as compared to socialist economies during the 1970s and 1980s.

7.	T	F	The *income ratio*, as a measure of the distribution of income in a society, tended to be higher in socialist systems as compared to capitalist systems during the 1970s and 1980s.
8.	T	F	More than two-thirds of employed men and women in the U.S. hold *white-collar jobs*.
9.	T	F	A larger percentage of workers today are *self-employed* as compared to any other period in the history of the United States.
10.	T	F	According to the text, the Information Revolution is changing the kind of work people do and where they do it. Part of the consequence of this process is that computers are *deskilling labor*.
11.	T	F	An *oligopoly* refers to domination of a market by a few producers.
12.	T	F	Corporations have grown so large that they now account for most of the world's economic output.

True-False--Politics

1.	T	F	*Authority* is power people perceive as legitimate rather than coercive.
2.	T	F	*Charismatic authority* is limited to the preindustrialized world.
3.	T	F	*Traditional authority* is sometimes referred to as bureaucratic authority.
4.	T	F	A political system giving power to the people as a whole is known as *democracy.*.
5.	T	F	*Authoritarianism* refers to a political system that denies popular participation in government.
6.	T	F	*Totalitarian* governments have spanned the political spectrum from fascist to communist.
7.	T	F	In the United States today, tax revenue, as a share of gross domestic product, is higher than in any other industrialized society.
8.	T	F	For every 13 U.S. citizens there is one government employee.
9.	T	F	Most U.S. adults claim identification with the *Republican Party*.
10.	T	F	*Political Action Committees* are organizations formed by special-interest groups, independent of political parties, to pursue political aims by raising and spending money.
11.	T	F	*Voter apathy* is a problem, as evidenced by the fact that citizens in the U.S. are less likely to vote today than they were a century ago.
12.	T	F	Research by *Robert* and *Helen Lynd* in Muncie, Indiana (the Middletown study) supported the *power-elite* model concerning how power is distributed in the United States.
13.	T	F	According to the *pluralist model* of U.S. politics, we are a democracy in which power is widely dispersed and in which apathy amounts to indifference.
14.	T	F	One of the four insights offered concerning *terrorism* is that democracies are especially vulnerable to it because these governments afford extensive civil liberties to their people and have limited police networks.
15.	T	F	In recent years, defense has been the largest single expenditure by the U.S. government, accounting for 19 percent of federal spending.

159

<u>Multiple Choice--Economics</u>

1. An organized sphere of social life, or societal subsystem designed to meet human needs is the definition for:

    (a)   social structure.
    (b)   social organization.
    (c)   social institution.
    (d)   corporation.

2. A productive system based on service work and extensive use of information technology refers to:

    (a)   the postindustrial economy.
    (b)   the primary sector.
    (c)   the secondary sector.
    (d)   a cottage industry.

3. The *sector* of the economy that transforms raw materials into manufactured goods is termed the:

    (a)   primary sector.
    (b)   competitive sector.
    (c)   secondary sector.
    (d)   basic sector.

4. Which of the following is *not a sector* of the modern economy?

    (a)   primary
    (b)   manifest
    (c)   secondary
    (d)   tertiary

5. Your occupation is teaching. In what production *sector* of the economy?

    (a)   primary
    (b)   secondary
    (c)   tertiary
    (d)   manifest

6. What is the *economic system* in which natural resources and the means of producing goods and services are privately owned?

    (a)   capitalism
    (b)   socialism
    (c)   communism
    (d)   state capitalism

7. Sweden and Italy represent what type of economic and political system?

   (a) capitalism
   (b) socialism
   (c) communism
   (d) welfare capitalism

8. An economic and political system that combines a mostly market-based economy with government programs to provide for people's basic needs is termed:

   (a) socialism.
   (b) market socialism.
   (c) market communism.
   (d) an oligarchy.
   (e) welfare capitalism.

9. An economic and political system in which companies are privately owned although they cooperate closely with the government is known as:

   (a) state socialism.
   (b) state capitalism.
   (c) welfare capitalism.
   (d) communism.

10. *Capitalist* economies had about _____ times the per capita GDP during the 1980s as *socialist* economies.

    (a) 2.7
    (b) 12.9
    (c) 8.2
    (d) .75
    (e) 1.3

11. During the 1970s and 1980s, *socialist economies* had about _____ as much *income inequality* as was found in capitalist economies during the same time period.

    (a) one-tenth
    (b) twice
    (c) three times
    (d) one-half
    (e) four times

12. By _____ a white-collar revolution had moved the majority of workers into *service occupations*.

   (a)   1900
   (b)   1930
   (c)   1950
   (d)   1975
   (e)   1990

13. By 2000, _____ percent of *new jobs* were in the *service sector*.

   (a)   50
   (b)   60
   (c)   70
   (d)   80
   (e)   90

14. In 1997, _____ percent of the U.S. labor force was *unionized*.

   (a)   less than 5
   (b)   about 14
   (c)   25
   (d)   36
   (e)   over 50

15. Currently, what percentage of the U.S. labor force is *self-employed*?

   (a)   less than 1
   (b)   3
   (c)   8
   (d)   15
   (e)   21

16. Which of the following statements is *most accurate*?

   (a)   White males have a much higher rate of unemployment than white females.
   (b)   A much higher proportion of African American females are unemployed than African American men.
   (c)   College graduates actually have a higher unemployment rate than the general population.
   (d)   The overall unemployment rate today in the U.S. is about ten percent.
   (e)   Teens have a higher rate of unemployment than people over the age of twenty.

17. What is the term for an organization with legal existence, including rights and liabilities, apart from those of its members?

    (a)   corporation
    (b)   bureaucracy
    (c)   business
    (d)   conglomerate

18. It is projected that by early in the twenty-first century, white, non-Hispanic males will represent _____ percent of the total U.S. work force.

    (a)   70
    (b)   58
    (c)   45
    (d)   33
    (e)   25

19. What is the term for giant corporations composed of many smaller corporations?

    (a)   megacorporations
    (b)   monopolies
    (c)   multinational corporations
    (d)   conglomerates
    (e)   oligarchies

20. Which U.S. corporation leads the nation in sales and assets?

    (a)   IBM
    (b)   General Motors
    (c)   Exxon
    (d)   Ford Motor Company
    (e)   Proctor and Gamble

21. What is the term for a social network made up of people who simultaneously serve on the board of directors of many corporations?

    (a)   conglomerate
    (b)   interlocking directorate
    (c)   oligopoly
    (d)   monopoly

22. The domination of a market by a single producer is called a(n):

    (a) conglomerate.
    (b) interlocking directorate.
    (c) monopoly.
    (d) oligopoly.

23. In 1996, the average *hourly wage* for a U.S. worker in manufacturing was $12.78. At $23.00 per hour, which country had the highest average wage for working in the manufacturing sector?

    (a) France
    (b) Russia
    (c) Canada
    (d) Germany
    (e) South Korea

24. Which of the following statements is/are accurate concerning the *economy of the twenty-first century* as reported in the text?

    (a) the share of the U.S. labor force engaged in manufacturing is now half of what is was in 1960
    (b) the global economy has shown that socialism is less productive than capitalism
    (c) the economic future of the U.S. and other nations will be played out in a global areans
    (d) the pressing challenge of global inequality must be addressed
    (e) all of the above

Multiple-Choice—Politics

1. Who defined *power* as the ability to achieve desired ends despite resistance?

    (a) C. Wright Mills
    (b) Max Weber
    (c) Alexis de Tocqueville
    (d) Robert Lynd

2. Power that people perceive as being *legitimate* rather than coercive is the definition for:

    (a) a monarchy.
    (b) totalitarianism.
    (c) government.
    (d) politics.
    (e) authority.

3. Which of the following is *not* one of the general contexts in which power is commonly defined as authority?

    (a)   traditional
    (b)   charismatic
    (c)   rational-legal
    (d)   democratic

4. Power that is legitimated by respect for long-established cultural patterns is called:

    (a)   traditional.
    (b)   sacred.
    (c)   political.
    (d)   charismatic.
    (e)   power-elite.

5. According to *Max Weber*, the survival of a charismatic movement depends upon _____.

    (a)   pluralism
    (b)   political action
    (c)   routinization
    (d)   assimilation

6. All the European societies whose *royal families* remain are:

    (a)   totalitarian democracies.
    (b)   authoritarian.
    (c)   constitutional monarchies.
    (d)   absolute monarchies.
    (e)   communist democracies.

7. What percentage of humanity live in nations that are classified as being *not free*?

    (a)   10
    (b)   20
    (c)   30
    (d)   39
    (e)   50

8. _____ refers to a political system that extensively regulates people's lives.

    (a)   Authoritarianism
    (b)   Totalitarianism
    (c)   Absolute monarchy
    (d)   State capitalism

9. Relatively speaking, which of the following nations has the largest government, based in tax revenues as a share of gross national product?

(a) Japan
(b) France
(c) the United States
(d) Canada
(e) Denmark

10. In 1998, the federal budget amounted to a *per capita* dollar amount of:

(a) 6,140.
(b) 1,100.
(c) 9,050.
(d) 780.

11. Which idea below represents the *pluralist model* of power?

(a) Power is highly concentrated.
(b) Voting cannot create significant political changes.
(c) The U.S. power system is an oligarchy.
(d) Power is widely dispersed throughout society.

12. With which general sociological paradigm is the *power-elite model* associated?

(a) social-conflict
(b) symbolic-interaction
(c) structural-functional
(d) social-exchange

13. An analysis that explains politics in terms of the operation of society's *economic system* is referred to as:

(a) pluralist theory.
(b) Marxist political-economy model.
(c) power-elite model.
(d) welfare state model.

14. In which stage of *revolution* does the danger of counter-revolution occur?

(a) rising expectations
(b) unresponsive government
(c) establishing a new legitimacy
(d) radical leadership by intellectuals

166

15. According to Paul Johnson, which of the following is/are distinguishing characteristics of *terrorism*?

    (a) Terrorists try to paint violence as a legitimate political tactic.
    (b) Terrorism is employed not just by groups, but by governments against their own people.
    (c) Democratic societies reject terrorism in principle, but they are especially vulnerable to terrorists because they afford extensive civil liberties.
    (d) Terrorism is always a matter of definition.
    (e) all of the above

16. *Quincy Wright* has identified which of the following circumstances as conditions which lead humans to go to war?

    (a) perceived threat
    (b) political objectives
    (c) social problems
    (d) moral objectives
    (e) all are identified

17. Together, the world's nations spend some _____ *trillion* annually for military purposes.

    (a) 5
    (b) 4
    (c) 1
    (d) 8
    (e) 2

18. *Military spending* accounts for _____ percent of the federal budget of the United States.

    (a) less than 5
    (b) 10
    (c) 19
    (d) 35
    (e) 50

19. Which of the following was *not* listed as a means of reducing the danger of nuclear war?

    (a) deterrence
    (b) high-technology defense
    (c) diplomacy and disarmament
    (d) resolving underlying conflict
    (e) all are identified

Matching--Economics

1. ____ A productive system based on service work and high technology.
2. ____ An economic and political system that combines a mostly market-based economy with government programs providing for people's basic needs.
3. ____ An economic system in which natural resources and the means of producing goods and services are collectively owned.
4. ____ The social institution that organizes a society's production, distribution, and consumption of goods and services.
5. ____ The part of the economy involving services rather than goods.
6. ____ Expanding economic activity with little regard for national borders.
7. ____ The part of the economy that transforms raw materials into manufactured goods.
8. ____ An organization with a legal existence, including rights and liabilities, apart from those of its members.
9. ____ Giant corporations composed of many smaller corporations.
10. ____ An economic and political system in which companies are privately owned although they cooperate closely with the government.

a.	socialism	f.	state capitalism
b.	conglomerates	g.	economy
c.	secondary sector	h.	postindustrial economy
d.	tertiary sector	i.	global economy
e.	welfare capitalism	j.	corporation

Matching--Politics

1. ____ Random acts of violence or the threat of such violence by an individual or group as a political strategy.
2. ____ A political system that extensively regulates people's lives.
3. ____ The ability to achieve desired ends despite resistance.
4. ____ An analysis of politics that views power as dispersed among many competing interest groups.
5. ____ The percentage adults in the U.S. who identify with the Republican party.
6. ____ Tax revenues as a share of the gross domestic product for Sweden in 1993.
7. ____ A political system that denies popular participation in government.
8. ____ An analysis of politics that views power as concentrated among the rich.
9. ____ Power people perceive as legitimate rather than coercive.
10. ____ Tax revenues as a share of the gross domestic product for the U.S. in 1994.

a.	power-elite model	f.	36.7
b.	31.7	g.	pluralist model
c.	authoritarianism	h.	power
d.	authority	i.	55.6
e.	terrorism	j.	totalitarianism

Fill-In--Economics

1. _____ range from necessities like food to luxuries like swimming pools, while _____ include various activities that benefit others.

2. *Industrialization* introduced five fundamental changes in the economies of Western societies, including: New forms of _____, the centralization of work in _____, manufacturing and _____ _____, _____, and _____ _____.

3. A _____ *economy* is a productive system based on service work and high technology.

4. The Information Revolution unleashed three key changes, including: From tangible products to _____, from mechanical skills to _____ skills, and from _____ to almost anywhere.

5. The _____ _____ is the part of the economy generating raw materials directly from the natural environment.

6. The _____ _____ is the part of the economy generating services rather than goods.

7. Four major consequences of a *global economy* include: Countries are becoming more _____; Products move through many _____; _____ governments no longer in control of their economies; And, _____ companies control more economic activity.

8. A *capitalist system* has three distinctive features, including: _____ ownership of property, pursuit of personal _____, and free _____ and consumer sovereignty.

9. A *socialist system* has three distinctive features, including: _____ ownership of property, pursuit of _____ goals, an _____ control of the economy.

10. _____ _____ is an economic and political system in which privately owned companies cooperate closely with the government.

11. _____ _____ is an economic and political system that combines a mostly market-based economy with government programs providing for people's basic needs.

12. A comparison of economic performance between *capitalist* and *socialist* economies supports the conclusion that capital economies produce a _____ overall standard of living but with _____ income disparity.

13. *Socialist* systems in Eastern Europe prior to the great transformations of 1989 and 1990 did do way with _____ *elites*, but expanded the clout of _____ *elites*.

14. While _____ percent of males over the age of 16 in the U.S. have income-producing jobs, _____ of the females do.

15. In Canada and Japan, about _____ percent of workers belong to *unions*; Across Europe, about _____ percent belong.

16. People describe their occupations as *professions* to the extent that they demonstrate the following four characteristics: _____ knowledge, _____ practice, _____ over clients, and _____ to community rather than to self-interest.

17. The *Information Revolution* is changing the kind of work people do as well as where they do it. Computers are altering the character of work in four additional ways: They are _____ labor, making work more _____ _____, _____ workplace interaction, and enhancing employer's _____ of workers.

169

18. _____ are giant corporations comprised of many smaller corporations.
19. _____ refers to domination of a market by a few producers.
20. *Dependency theorists* argue that multinationals _____ global inequality.

Fill-In--Politics

1. _____ is the social institution that distributes power, sets a social agenda, and makes decisions.
2. *Power* people perceive as legitimate rather than coercive is referred to as _____.
3. Max Weber differentiated between three types of *authority*, including _____, _____, and _____.
4. _____ *authority* is power legitimated through extraordinary personal abilities that inspire devotion and obedience.
5. _____ is a political system giving power to the people as a whole..
6. A _____ is a political system in which a single family rules from generation to generation.
7. _____ is a political system that denies popular participation in government.
8. A _____ _____ refers to a range of government agencies and programs that provides benefits to the population.
9. One major cluster of attitudes related to the *political spectrum* concerns _____ issues, while another concerns _____ issues.
10. In 1996, while 36.7 percent of the adult population identified with the *Republican Party*, _____ identified with the *Democratic Party*.
11. _____ _____ _____ are organizations formed by a special-interest group, independent of political parties, to pursue political aims by raising and spending money.
12. While conservatives suggest *voter apathy* amounts to an _____ to politics, liberals counter that most non-voters are _____ from politics.
13. The _____ *model*, closely allied with the *social-conflict paradigm*, is an analysis of politics that views power as concentrated among the rich.
14. The _____ _____ *model* is an analysis that explains politics in terms of the operation of a society's economic system.
15. Analysts claim *revolutions* share a number of traits, including: rising _____, _____ government, _____ leadership by intellectuals, and establishing a new _____.
16. According to Paul Johnson, *terrorism* has four distinguishing characteristics, including: Terrorists try to paint violence as a _____ political tactic, terrorism is employed not just by groups, but also by _____ against their own people, democratic societies reject terrorism in principle, but they are especially _____ to terrorists because they afford extensive civil liberties to their people, and terrorism is always a matter of _____.
17. *Quincy Wright* cites five factors that promote *war*, including: perceived _____, social _____, _____ objectives, _____imperatives, and the absence of _____.

18.   The most recent approaches to *peace* include: _____, high-technology _____, _____ and disarmament, and resolving underlying _____.

Definition and Short-Answer-Economics

1.   What were the five revolutionary changes brought about by the *Industrial Revolution*?
2.   Define the concept *postindustrial society*, and identify three key changes unleashed by the *Information Revolution*.
3.   What are the three basic characteristics of *capitalism*?
4.   What are the three basic characteristics of *socialism*?
5.   What is *democratic socialism*?
6.   Comparing productivity and economic equality measures for *capitalist* and *socialist* economic systems, what are the relative advantages and disadvantages of each? Make comparisons in terms of *productivity, economic inequality,* and *civil liberties.*
7.   What are the three main consequences of the development of a *global economy*?
8.   What are the three major *sectors* of the economy? Define and illustrate each of these.
9.   What are the basic characteristics of a *profession*?

Definition and Short-Answer--Politics

1.   Differentiate between the concepts *power* and *authority.*
2.   Differentiate between *Max Weber's* three types of *authority.*
3.   Four types of *political systems* are reviewed in the text. Identify and describe each of these systems.
4.   What are the general patterns in attitudes among U.S. citizens concerning *social* and *economic issues* as reviewed in the text?
5.   What is the evidence that *voter apathy* is a problem in our society? What are its causes?
6.   Discuss the *changing work place* using demographic data presented in the text. What are three changes that you think are positive? What are three changes you think are negative?
7.   Differentiate between the *pluralist* and *power-elite* models concerning the distribution of power in the United States.
8.   What are the five general patterns identified in the text concerning *revolutions*?
9.   What are the five factors identified in the text as promoting *war*?
10.   Several approaches to reducing the chances for *nuclear war* are addressed in the text. Identify these approaches.
11.   In what three ways has politics gone global?
12.   What are the five insights presented in the text concerning *terrorism*?

PART VI: ANSWERS TO STUDY QUESTIONS

True-False--Economics

1.	T	(p. 274)	7.	F	(p. 280)
2.	T	(p. 274)	8.	T	(p. 281)
3.	T	(p. 275)	9.	F	(p. 283)

4.	F	(p. 275)		10.	T	(p. 284)
5.	F	(p. 278)		11.	T	(p. 286)
6.	T	(p. 280)		12.	T	(p. 286)

True-False—Politics

1.	T	(p. 288)		9.	F	(p. 294)
2.	F	(pp. 288-289)		10.	T	(p. 294)
3.	F	(p. 288)		11.	T	(p. 294)
4.	T	(p. 289)		12.	T	(p. 295)
5.	T	(p. 289)		13.	T	(p. 295
6.	T	(p. 290)		14.	T	(p. 298)
7.	F	(p. 292)		15.	T	(p. 299)
8.	T	(pp. 292-293)				

Multiple-Choice--Economics

1.	c	(p. 274)		13.	e	(p. 281)
2.	a	(p. 275)		14.	b	(p. 282)
3.	c	(p. 275)		15.	c	(p. 283)
4.	b	(p. 275)		16.	e	(p. 284)
5.	c	(p. 275)		17.	a	(p. 285)
6.	a	(p. 278)		18.	c	(p. 285)
7.	d	(p. 279)		19.	d	(p. 285)
8.	e	(p. 279)		20.	b	(p. 286)
9.	b	(p. 279)		21.	b	(p. 286)
10.	a	(p. 280)		22.	c	(p. 286)
11.	d	(p. 280)		23.	d	(p. 286)
12.	c	(p. 281)		24.	e	(pp. 287-288)

Multiple-Choice--Politics

1.	b	(p. 288)		11.	d	(p. 295)
2.	e	(p. 288)		12.	a	(p. 295)
3.	d	(p. 288)		13.	b	(p. 296)
4.	a	(p. 288)		14.	c	(p. 297)
5.	c	(p. 289)		15.	e	(p. 298)
6.	c	(p. 289)		16.	e	(p. 299)
7.	d	(p. 291)		17.	a	(p. 299)
8.	b	(p. 290)		18.	c	(p. 299)
9.	e	(p. 292)		19.	e	(pp. 300-301)
10.	a	(p. 292)				

Matching--Economics

1.	h	(p. 275)	6.	i.	(p. 276)
2.	e	(p. 279)	7.	c	(p. 275)
3.	a	(p. 278)	8.	j	(p. 285)
4.	g	(p. 274)	9.	b	(p. 286)
5.	d	(p. 275)	10.	f	(p. 279)

Matching-Politics

1.	e	(p. 298)	6.	i.	(p. 292)
2.	j.	(p. 290)	7.	c	(p. 289)
3.	h	(p. 304)	8.	a	(p. 295)
4.	g	(p. 295)	9.	d	(p. 288)
5.	f	(p. 294)	10.	b	(p. 292)

Fill-In--Economics

1. goods, services (p. 274)
2. energy, factories, mass production, specialization, wage labor (p. 274)
3. postindustrial (p. 275)
4. ideas, literacy, factories (p. 275)
5. primary sector (p. 275)
6. tertiary sector (p. 275)
7. specialization, countries, national, large (p. 275)
8. private, profit, competition (p. 278)
9. collective, collective, government (p. 278)
10. State capitalism (p. 279)
11. Welfare capitalism (p. 279)
12. higher, greater (p. 280)
13. economic, political (p. 281)
14. 75, 59.8 (p. 281)
15. 33, 40 (p. 282)
16. theoretical, self-regulating, authority, orientation (p. 282)
17. deskilling, abstract, limiting, control (p. 284)
18. Conglomerates (p. 286)
19. Oligopoly (p. 286)
20. intensify (p. 287)

Fill-In--Politics

1. politics (p. 288)
2. authority (p. 288)
3. traditional, rational-legal, charismatic (p. 288)
4. charismatic (p. 288)

173

5. Democracy (p. 289)
6. monarchy (p. 289)
7. authoritarianism (p. 289)
8. welfare state (p. 292)
9. economic, social (p. 293)
10. 46 (p. 294)
11. Political Action Committees (p. 294)
12. indifference, alienation (p. 294)
13. power-elite (p. 295)
14. Marxist political-economy (p. 296)
15. expectations, unresponsive, radical, legitimacy (p. 297)
16. legitimate, governments, vulnerable, definition (p. 298)
17. threat, problems, political, moral, alternatives (p. 299)
18. deterrence, defense, diplomacy, conflict (pp. 300-301)

PART VII: IN FOCUS—IMPORTANT ISSUES

- Identify five major change brought about by the *Industrial Revolution*.

- Identify three changes brought about by the *Information Revolution*.

- Define and illustrate each of the following three *sectors of the economy*.

    Primary:

    Secondary:

    Tertiary:

- Identify the four main consequences of the development of a *global economy*.

- Define and identify the distinctive features of each of the following *economic systems*.

  Capitalism:

  Socialism:

- What are four ways in which *new information technology* has affected work in our economy? Provide an illustration for each.

- Define each of the following *political systems*.

  Monarchy: Democracy:

  Authoritarian: Totalitarian:

- Differentiate between the following models.

  Pluralist:

  Power-Elite:

  Marxist:

- Identify the four major *stages of a revolution:*

- Identify five factors that *promote war:*

- What are four *approaches for promoting peace?*

PART VIII: ANALYSIS AND COMMENT

Social Diversity

"Work Force 2000: The Trend Toward Diversity"

Key Points: Questions:

Exploring Cyber-Society

"On-Line Democracy: Can Computers Increase Political Participation?"

Key Points: Questions:

Controversy and Debate

"Information Warfare: Let Your Fingers Do the Fighting"

Key Points: Questions:

Window on the World--Global Map 11-1, 11-2

"Agricultural Employment in Global Perspective"

Key Points: Questions:

"Industrial Employment in Global Perspective"

Key Points: Questions:

Seeing Ourselves--National Map 11-1

"Labor Force Participation across the United States"

Key Points: Questions:

177

12 Family and Religion

PART I: CHAPTER OUTLINE

I.   The Family: Basic Concepts
II.   The Family: Global Variations
    A.   Marriage Patterns
    B.   Residential Patterns
    C.   Patterns of Descent
    D.   Patterns of Authority
III. Theoretical Analysis of the Family
    A.   Functions of the Family: Structural-Functional Analysis
    B.   Inequality and the Family: Social-Conflict Analysis
    C.   Constructing Family Life: Micro-Level Analysis
IV.   Stages of Family Life
    A.   Courtship and Romantic Love
    B.   Settling In: Ideal and Real Marriage
    C.   Child Rearing
    D.   The Family in Later Life
V.   U.S. Families: Class, Race, and Gender
    A.   Social Class
    B.   Ethnicity and Race
    C.   Gender
VI.   Transitions and Problems in Family Life
    A.   Divorce
    B.   Remarriage
    C.   Family Violence
VII. Alternative Family Forms
    A.   One-Parent Families
    B.   Cohabitation
    C.   Gay and Lesbian Couples
    D.   Singlehood
    E.   New Reproductive Technology
    F.   Looking Ahead: The Family in the Twenty-First Century

PART II: LEARNING OBJECTIVES

1. To be able to define and illustrate basic concepts relating to the social institutions of kinship, family, and marriage.
2. To gain a cross-cultural perspectives of the social institutions of kinship, family, and marriage.
3. To be able to analyze the social institutions of kinship, family, and marriage using the structural-functional, social-conflict, and symbolic-interaction perspectives.
4. To be able to describe the traditional life course of the U.S. family.
5. To be able to recognize the impact of social class, race, ethnicity, and gender socialization on the family.
6. To be able describe the problems and transitions that seriously affect family life.
7. To be able to describe the composition and prevalence of alternative family forms.
8. To become aware of the impact, both technologically and ethically, of new reproductive techniques on the family.
9. To be able to identify four sociological conclusions about the family as we enter the twenty-first century.
10. To be able to define basic concepts relating to the sociological analysis of religion.
11. To be able to identify and describe the three functions of religion as developed by Emile Durkheim.
12. To be able to discuss the view that religion is socially constructed.
13. To be able to discuss the role of religion in maintaining social inequality.

14. To be able to describe how industrialization and science affect religious beliefs and practices.
15. To be able to compare and contrast the basic types of religious organization.
16. To be able to distinguish between preindustrial and industrial societies in terms of religious beliefs and practices.
17. To be able to discuss the basic demographic patterns concerning religious affiliation, religiosity, secularization, and religious revival in the U.S. today.
18. To begin to critically think about the role of religion in the world as it will unfold over the next generation, and to consider the relationship between religion and science.

PART III: KEY CONCEPTS

Family:

bilateral descent
cohabitation
conjugal family
consanguine family
descent
endogamy
extended family
family
family of affinity
family of orientation
family of procreation
family unit
family violence
homogamy
incest taboo
in vitro fertilization
kinship
marriage
matrilineal descent
matrilocality
monogamy
neolocality
nuclear family
patrilineal descent
patrilocality
polyandry
polygamy
polygyny
romantic love

Religion:

animism
bodhi
charisma
church
civil religion
conversion
creationism
creation science
cult
denomination
dhamma
dharma
ecclesia
faith
fundamentalism
karma
liberation theology
profane
religion
religiosity
ritual
sacred
sect
secularism
Torah
totem

PART IV: IMPORTANT RESEARCHERS

Lillian Rubin   Jessie Bernard

Max Weber   Emile Durkheim

Karl Marx

PART V: STUDY QUESTIONS

True-False--Family

1.	T	F	*Families of affinity* are comprised of people related by blood.
2.	T	F	Because it is based on marriage, the nuclear family is also known as the *conjugal family*.
3.	T	F	Norms of *endogamy* relate to marriage between people of the same social category.
4.	T	F	*Matrilocality* occurs more commonly in societies that engage in distant warfare or in which daughters have greater economic value.
5.	T	F	*Polyandry* is much more common around the world than is *polygyny*.
6.	T	F	*Neolocality* refers to a residential pattern in which a married couple lives apart from the parents of both spouses.
7.	T	F	Every known culture has some type of *incest taboo*.
8.	T	F	Our society places less of an emphasis on *romantic love* than most other cultures around the world.
9.	T	F	Economically speaking, industrialization transforms children from an asset to a *liability*.
10.	T	F	While the actual number is smaller, the "ideal" number of children to have for most married U.S. adults is three or more.
11.	T	F	Most children under the age of five whose parent(s) work outside of the home in paid employment attend organized *day care* or *preschool* programs.
12.	T	F	Over forty-five percent of African American families are *headed by women*.
13.	T	F	*Jessie Bernard's* research on marriage suggests that this institution is more beneficial for men than it is for women.
14.	T	F	The *divorce rate* in the U.S. during the twentieth century has actually only increased by less than 30 percent.
15.	T	F	While the *divorce rate* is in the U.S. high, relative to other industrialized societies it is fairly low.
16.	T	F	*Blended families* are composed of children and some combination of biological parents and stepparents.
17.	T	F	According to the text, most *child abusers* are men.
18.	T	F	Same-sex marriage are *legal* in most of the United States.
19.	T	F	The percentage of households with *single adults* has actually been decreasing over the last two decades.
20.	T	F	*Test-tube babies* are, technically speaking, the result of the process of *in vitro fertilization*.

<u>True-False--Religion</u>

1.	T	F	The *profane* refers to that, which is an ordinary element of everyday life.
2.	T	F	Emile Durkheim defined a *totem* as an object in the natural world collectively defined as sacred.
3.	T	F	According to Emile Durkheim, society has an existence and power of its own, beyond the lives of the people who collectively created it.
4.	T	F	A major criticism of Emile Durkheim's analysis of religion is that he focuses too much attention on the *dysfunctions* of religious belief and practice.
5.	T	F	The symbolic-interaction approach views religion as a *social construction*.
6.	T	F	Social-conflict theory focuses on how religion promotes change and equality.
7.	T	F	*Liberation theology* is a fusion of Christian principles with political activism, often Marxist in character.
8.	T	F	Two types, or forms, of churches identified in the text are the *ecclesia* and the *denomination*.
9.	T	F	Whereas a *cult* is a type of religious organization that stands apart from the larger society, a *sect* represents something almost entirely new and stands outside a society's cultural tradition.
10.	T	F	*Animism* is the belief that natural objects are conscious life forms that affect humanity.
11.	T	F	Religious organization in the U.S. is defined as *ecclesiastical*.
12.	T	F	Our society is as *religiously diverse* as any on earth.
13.	T	F	Fewer than 40 percent of people in the United States identify with a religion.
14.	T	F	*Religiosity* refers to the importance of religion in a person's life.
15.	T	F	By global standards, *North Americans* are relatively nonreligious people.
16.	T	F	*Religious affiliation* does not vary much in the U.S. by social class.
17.	T	F	A quasi-religious loyalty based in citizenship is called a *civil religion*.
18.	T	F	In a recent national survey, almost one-third of U.S. adults described their religious upbringing as *fundamentalist*.
19.	T	F	Science and new technologies are reducing the relevance of religion in modern society as many moral dilemmas and spiritual issues are resolved or are diminishing in significance.
20.	T	F	The *Scopes Monkey Trial* of 1925 involved the prosecution of a science teacher who was teaching evolution in violation to Tennessee state law.

<u>Multiple Choice--Family</u>

1.   A _____ refers to a family unit composed of one or two adults and their children.

    (a)   kinship group
    (b)   nuclear family
    (c)   marriage
    (d)   consanguine family

2.	_____ refers to a social bond, based on blood, marriage or adoption, that joins individuals into families?

(a)	Descent group
(b)	Nuclear family
(c)	Family
(d)	Kinship

3.	The *consanguine family* is also known as the:

(a)	conjugal family.
(b)	family of orientation.
(c)	nuclear family.
(d)	family of procreation.
(e)	extended family.

4.	What is the family unit including parents and children, but also other kin?

(a)	a family
(b)	a kinship group
(c)	a nuclear family
(d)	an extended family

5.	Which of the following cultural norms promotes the pattern of marriage between people of the same social category?

(a)	endogamy
(b)	monogamy
(c)	exogamy
(d)	polygamy

6.	Marriage between people of different social categories is called:

(a)	polygamy.
(b)	monogamy.
(c)	exogamy.
(d)	endogamy.

7.	What is a marriage that joins *one female* with *more than one male*?

(a)	polygamy
(b)	polyandry
(c)	endogamy
(d)	polygyny

8.   What is the residential pattern in which a married couple lives apart from the parents of both spouses?

(a)   neolocality
(b)   patrilocality
(c)   matrilocality
(d)   avunculocality
(e)   bilateral descent

9.   What is the system by which members of a society trace kinship over generations?

(a)   descent
(b)   family
(c)   marriage
(d)   extended family

10.   The type of sociological analysis of the family that holds that the family serves to perpetuate social inequality is:

(a)   social-exchange analysis.
(b)   structural-functional analysis.
(c)   social-conflict analysis.
(d)   symbolic-interaction analysis.

11.   Which theory and theorist traced the origin of the family to the need for men to pass property on to their sons?

(a)   symbolic-interaction--George Herbert Mead
(b)   structural-functionalism--Talcott Parsons
(c)   structural-functionalism--Emile Durkheim
(d)   social-conflict--Friedrich Engels

12.   Which of the following is *not* one of the ways that families aid in the perpetuation of social inequality?

(a)   property and inheritance
(b)   bilineal descent
(c)   patriarchy
(d)   race and ethnicity

13.   The depiction of courtship and marriage as forms of negotiation is found in the _____ *analysis*.

(a)   structural-functional
(b)   social-conflict
(c)   symbolic-interaction
(d)   social-exchange

14. Sociologists have noted that *romantic love* as a basis for marriage:

    (a) is reinforced by cultural values.
    (b) acts as a strong incentive to leave one's original family of orientation to form a new family of procreation.
    (c) is not as stable a basis for marriage as social and economic bases.
    (d) all of the above

15. Most adults in the U.S. feel the *ideal number* of children is:

    (a) 1.
    (b) 2.
    (c) 3.
    (d) 4.

16. Which of the following is *not* one of the familial adjustments made by parents in *later life*?

    (a) adjustment to retirement and spending more time together
    (b) helping to care for grandchildren
    (c) assumption of more household responsibilities
    (d) death of a spouse

17. Lillian Rubin focused her research on the relationship between _____ and marriage.

    (a) social class
    (b) race
    (c) presence of children
    (d) age at marriage

18. Which group has the proportionately highest number of *single heads-of-households*?

    (a) African Americans
    (b) Hispanics
    (c) Asian Americans
    (d) whites

19. Which of the following is *not* a finding of Jessie Bernard's study of marriage?

    (a) married women have poorer mental health
    (b) married women have more passive attitudes toward life
    (c) married women report less personal happiness
    (d) married women are not generally required to participate in the labor force

20. Remarriage often creates families composed of both biological parents and stepparents and children. These are called:

    (a)   second families.
    (b)   blended families.
    (c)   focal families.
    (d)   families of orientation.

21. In the U.S. annually, there are approximately _____ *reported cases* of child abuse and neglect?

    (a)   about 100,000
    (b)   6 million
    (c)   two million
    (d)   300,000

22. Which country, in 1989, became the first nation to legalize *same-sex marriages*?

    (a)   Denmark
    (b)   France
    (c)   the United States
    (d)   Japan

Multiple Choice--Religion

1. Formal, ceremonial behavior refers to:

    (a)   the sacred.
    (b)   ritual.
    (c)   religion.
    (d)   faith.

2. What is the term for the social institution involving beliefs and practices based upon a conception of the sacred?

    (a)   faith
    (b)   totem
    (c)   religion
    (d)   ritual

3. Emile Durkheim referred to the ordinary elements of everyday life as:

    (a)   religion.
    (b)   faith
    (c)   ritual.
    (d)   the profane.

4. Which of the following is a function of religion according to *Emile Durkheim*?

   (a)   social cohesion
   (b)   social control
   (c)   providing meaning and purpose
   (d)   all are functions identified by Durkheim
   (e)   none are, as he saw religion as having negative consequences for society

5. The view that religion is completely *socially constructed* by a society's members is espoused by:

   (a)   Max Weber.
   (b)   Peter Berger.
   (c)   Karl Marx.
   (d)   Emile Durkheim.

6. Which of the following is an appropriate criticism of a *symbolic-interactionist* approach to religion:

   (a)   It ignores religion's link to inequality.
   (b)   It fails to consider the importance of rituals.
   (c)   It treats reality as objective.
   (d)   It ignores the social construction of religion.

7. Who would be most likely to argue that religion motivates *capitalism*?

   (a)   a Marxist
   (b)   a symbolic interactionist
   (c)   a follower of Max Weber
   (d)   a person following the precepts of liberation theology

8. *Liberation theology* advocates a blending of religion with:

   (a)   the family.
   (b)   the economy.
   (c)   education.
   (d)   politics.

9. A church that is formally allied with the state is called a(n):

   (a)   church.
   (b)   denomination.
   (c)   ecclesia.
   (d)   sect.
   (e)   cult.

10. Which of the following is *not* a feature of a *sect*:

    (a) charismatic leaders
    (b) psychic intensity and informal structure
    (c) membership through conversion
    (d) proselytizing
    (e) all of the above are features of a sect

11. A religious organization that is substantially outside society's cultural tradition is called a:

    (a) totem.
    (b) cult.
    (c) ecclesia.
    (d) sect.

12. The belief that elements of the natural world are conscious life forms that affect humanity refers to:

    (a) animism.
    (b) cults.
    (c) a totem.
    (d) sects.

13. Which of the following is the largest *Protestant denomination*?

    (a) Baptist
    (b) Presbyterian
    (c) Methodist
    (d) Episcopalian
    (e) Lutheran

14. What percentage of U.S. adults consider themselves *Protestants*?

    (a) 24
    (b) 35
    (c) 57
    (d) 78

15. Which of the following is most accurate?

    (a) Baptists and Lutherans have lower social standing compared to members of other denominations.
    (b) Religion is not tied to ethnicity in any way.
    (c) Religiosity does not seem to vary among denominations.
    (d) Sixty percent of U.S. adults regularly attend church.

16. What is *secularization?*

    (a) the ecumenical movement
    (b) the historical decline in the importance the supernatural and the sacred
    (c) the increase in religiosity in postindustrial society
    (d) fundamentalism

17. A quasi-religious loyalty binding individuals in a basically secular society is referred to as:

    (a) a totem.
    (b) secularization.
    (c) religiosity.
    (d) fundamentalism.
    (e) civil religion.

18. In the *Scopes trial* of 1925, the state of Tennessee prosecuted a man for:

    (a) polygamy.
    (b) profanity.
    (c) cohabitation.
    (d) teaching evolution.

Matching--Family

1. _____ The system by which members of a society trace kinship over generations.
2. _____ People with or without legal or blood ties who feel they belong together and want to define themselves as a family.
3. _____ Marriage between people of the same social category.
4. _____ Families composed of children and some combination of biological parents and stepparents.
5. _____ A family unit including parents, children, but also other kin.
6. _____ A residential pattern in which a married couple lives apart from the parents of both spouses.
7. _____ A form of marriage uniting one female with more than one male.
8. _____ A system tracing kinship through both men and women.
9. _____ The feeling of affection and sexual passion toward another person as the basis of marriage.
10. _____ A form of marriage uniting one male with more than one female.

a.	endogamy	f.	neolocality
b.	extended family	g.	family of affinity
c.	blended families	h.	polygyny
d.	bilateral decent	i.	polyandry
e.	descent	j.	romantic love

Matching--Religion

1. ___ That which is an ordinary element of everyday life.
2. ___ The social institution involving beliefs and practices based upon a conception of the sacred.
3. ___ Belief anchored in conviction rather than scientific evidence.
4. ___ An object in the natural world collectively defined as sacred.
5. ___ Suggested that the religious doctrine of Calvinism sparked the Industrial Revolution in Western Europe.
6. ___ A type of religious organization well integrated into the larger society.
7. ___ Extraordinary personal qualities that can turn an audience into followers.
8. ___ A church formally allied with the state.
9. ___ A type of religious organization that stands apart from the larger society.
10. ___ A religious organization that is substantially outside a society's cultural traditions.
11. ___ The importance of religion in a person's life.
12. ___ The historical decline in the importance of the supernatural and the sacred.
13. ___ A conservative religious doctrine that opposes intellectualism and worldly accommodation in favor of restoring traditional, otherworldly spirituality.

a.	ecclesia	i.	church
b.	fundamentalism	j.	faith
c.	religiosity	k.	totem
d.	religion	l.	secularization
e.	charisma	m.	cult
f.	profane	n.	Max Weber
g.	civil religion	o.	Emile Durkheim
h.	sacred	p.	sect

Fill-In--Family

1. The _____ is a social institution that unites individuals into cooperative groups that oversee the bearing and raising of children.
2. More and more organizations are coming to recognize families of _____, that is, people with or without legal or blood ties who feel they belong together and want to define themselves as a family.
3. _____ refers to a social bond, based on blood, marriage, or adoption, that joins individuals into families.
4. The _____ *family* is based on blood ties.
5. _____ refers to marriage between people of the same social group or category.
6. _____ is a marriage that joins one female with more than one male.
7. _____ refers to the system by which members of a society trace kinship over generations.
8. _____ *descent* is a system tracing kinship through both men and women.
9. Structural-functionalists identify several *vital tasks* performed by the family. These include: _____, _____ of sexual activity, social _____, and material and economic _____,

191

10. Cultural norms that forbid sexual relationships or marriage between specified kin are called _____ _____.

11. *Social-conflict* theorists argue that families perpetuate social inequality in several ways, including: Property and _____, _____, and _____ and _____.

12. Our culture celebrates _____ _____--the feeling of affection and sexual passion toward another person--as the basis for marriage.

13. About _____ of U.S. children under the age of five whose mothers work outside the home in paid employment spend time in *organized child-care facilities*.

14. Women headed _____ *percent* of African American families in 1998.

15. Jessie Bernard suggests that every marriage is actually _____ different relationships.

16. The high U.S. *divorce rate* has many causes, including: _____ is on the rise, _____ _____ often subsides, women are now less _____ on men, many of today's marriages are _____, divorce is more socially _____, and from a legal standpoint, divorce is _____ to obtain.

17. Remarriage often creates _____ *families*, composed of children and some combination of biological parents and stepparents.

18. The FBI estimates that at least _____ women are victims of *domestic violence* each year in he United States.

19. Today, _____ states have enacted *marital rape laws*.

20. *Family violence* includes _____, _____, or _____ abuse of one family member by another.

21. _____ is the sharing of a household by an unmarried couple.

22. *Test-tube babies* are the result of _____ _____ _____.

23. Sociologists point our five probable *future trends* regarding the family. These include: _____ rates are likely to remain high, family life will be highly _____, men are likely to continue to play a limited role in _____ _____, we will continue to feel the effects of _____ changes in our families, and the importance of new _____ technology will increase.

Fill-In—Religion

1. *Emile Durkheim* labeled the ordinary elements of everyday life the _____.

2. A _____ is a natural object—or its representation—collectively defined as sacred.

3. _____ refers to belief anchored in conviction rather than scientific evidence.

4. According to *Emile Durkheim*, three major *functions of religion* include: Social _____, social _____, and providing _____ and _____.

5. According to *Max Weber*, industrial capitalism developed in the wake of _____.

6. _____ *theology* is a fusion of Christian principles with political activism.

7. A(n) _____ is a church that is formally allied with the state.

8. _____ refers to extraordinary personal qualities that can turn audiences into followers.

9. _____ is the belief that natural objects are conscious forms of life that can affect humanity.

10. _____ refers to the importance of religion in a person's life.

11. _____ *percent* of U.S. adults state no religious preference.
12. The historical decline in the importance of the supernatural and the sacred is referred to as _____ .
13. A _____ religion is a quasi-religious loyalty based on citizenship.
14. _____ refers to a conservative religious doctrine that opposes intellectualism and worldly accommodation in favor of restoring traditional, otherworldly spirituality.
15. *Religious fundamentalism* is distinctive in five ways, including: interpreting sacred texts _____ , rejecting religious _____ , pursuing the personal experience of God's _____ , opposition to secular _____ , and endorsement of _____ political goals.

Definition and Short-Answer

1. What are the four basic *functions* of the family according to structural-functionalists?
2. Define and describe the three patterns of *descent*.
3. Why has the *divorce rate* increased in recent decades in the United States? What are the basic demographic patterns involving divorce in our society today?
4. What are the four *stages* of the family life cycle outlined in the text? Describe the major events occurring during each of these stages.
5. In what ways are *middle-class* and *working-class* marriages different?
6. What are the arguments being made about the family by *social-conflict* theorists?
7. What are four important points made in the text concerning *family violence*?
8. Five *alternative family forms* are discussed in the text. Identify these and review the data concerning three of them. What are your opinions concerning these changes in the family?
9. What are the five conclusions being made about marriage and family life into the twenty-first century?
10. What are the dimensions of *family violence*? What are the demographic patterns concerning each of these?
11. According to *structural-functional* analysis, what are three major functions of religion? Provide an example for each from U.S. society.
12. Discuss *Max Weber's* points concerning the historical relationship between *Protestantism* and *capitalism*.
13. How do theorists operating from the *social conflict* perspective understand religion and how it operates in society? Provide two examples to illustrate.
14. In a one-page written discussion, debate the issue of whether science threatens or strengthens religion in society.
15. Discuss the issue concerning the extent of *religiosity* in the United States today.
16. Briefly describe the position of religious *fundamentalism* in our society today.
17. Discuss the relationship between *religion* and *social stratification* in the United States today.
18. Differentiate between the nature of religion in *preindustrial* and *industrial* societies.
19. Differentiate between *civil religion* and *religious fundamentalism*.

PART VI: ANSWERS TO STUDY QUESTIONS

True-False--Family

1.	F	(p. 308)	11.	F	(p. 315)
2.	T	(p. 308)	12.	T	(p. 315)
3.	T	(p. 309)	13.	T	(p. 318)
4.	T	(p. 309)	14.	F	(pp. 318-319)
5.	F	(p. 309)	15.	F	(p. 319)
6.	T	(p. 309)	16.	T	(p. 320)
7.	T	(p. 311)	17.	T	(p. 321)
8.	F	(p. 313)	18.	F	(p. 322)
9.	T	(p. 315)	19.	F	(p. 323)
10.	F	(p. 315)	20.	T	(p. 323)

True-False--Religion

1.	T	(p. 326)	11.	T	(p. 331)
2.	T	(p. 326)	12.	F	(p. 331)
3.	T	(p. 326)	13.	F	(p. 331)
4.	F	(p. 326)	14.	T	(p. 332)
5.	T	(p. 327)	15.	F	(p. 331)
6.	F	(p. 327)	16.	F	(p. 332)
7.	T	(p. 329)	17.	T	(p. 333)
8.	T	(p. 329)	18.	T	(p. 334)
9.	F	(p. 330)	19.	F	(p. 336)
10.	T	(p. 331)	20.	T	(p. 336)

Multiple Choice--Family

1.	b	(p. 308)	12.	b	(pp. 311-312)
2.	d	(p. 308)	13.	d	(p. 312)
3.	e	(p. 308)	14.	d	(p. 313)
4.	d	(p. 308)	15.	b	(p. 315)
5.	a	(p. 309)	16.	c	(pp. 315-316)
6.	c	(p. 309)	17.	a	(p. 316)
7.	b	(p. 309)	18.	a	(p. 317)
8.	a	(p. 309)	19.	d	(p. 318)
9.	a	(p. 310)	20.	b	(p. 320)
10.	c	(p. 311)	21.	c	(p. 321)
11.	d	(p. 311)	22.	a	(p. 323)

Multiple Choice--Religion

1.	b	(p. 326)
2.	c	(p. 326)
3.	d	(p. 326)
4.	d	(p. 327)
5.	b	(p. 327)
6.	a	(p. 327)
7.	c	(p. 328)
8.	d	(p. 329)
9.	c	(p. 329)
10.	e	(p. 330)
11.	b	(p. 330)
12.	a	(p. 331)
13.	c	(p. 330)
14.	c	(p. 331)
15.	a	(p. 332)
16.	b	(p. 333)
17.	e	(p. 333)
18.	d	(p. 336)

Matching--Family

1.	e	(p. 310)
2.	g	(p. 308)
3.	a	(p. 309)
4.	c	(p. 320)
5.	b	(p. 308)
6.	f	(p. 309)
7.	i.	(p. 309)
8.	d	(p. 311)
9.	j	(p. 313)
10.	h	(p. 309)

Matching--Religion

1.	f	(p. 326)
2.	d	(p. 326)
3.	j	(p. 326)
4.	k	(p. 327)
5.	n	(p. 328)
6.	i	(p. 329)
7.	e	(p. 330)
8.	a	(p. 329)
9.	p	(p. 330)
10.	m	(p. 330)
11.	c	(p. 332)
12.	l	(p. 333)
13.	b	(p. 334)

Fill-In--Family

1. family (p. 308)
2. affinity (p. 308)
3. Kinship (p. 308)
4. consanguine (p. 308)
5. endogamy (p. 309)
6. Polyandry (p. 309)
7. Descent (p. 310)
8. Bilateral (p. 311)
9. socialization, regulation, placement, security (p. 311)
10. incest taboos (p. 311)
11. inheritance, patriarchy, race, ethnicity (pp. 311-312)
12. romantic love (p. 313)
13. one-third (p. 315)

14. 47 (p. 316)
15. two (p. 318)
16. individualism, romantic love, dependent, stressful, acceptable, easier (p. 319)
17. blended (p. 320)
18. 600,000 (p. 321)
19. all (p. 321)
20. emotional, physical, sexual (pp. 320-321)
21. Cohabitation (p. 322)
22. in vitro fertilization (p. 323)
23. divorce, variable, child rearing, economic, reproductive (pp. 324-325)

Fill-In

1. profane (p. 326)
2. totem (p. 327)
3. faith (p. 326)
4. cohesion, control meaning, purpose (p. 327)
5. Calvinism (p. 328)
6. Liberation (p. 329)
7. ecclesia (p. 329)
8. charisma (p. 330)
9. animism (p. 331)
10. Religiosity (p. 332)
11. 11.7 (p. 330)
12. secularization (p. 333)
13. civil (p. 333)
14. fundamentalism (p. 334)
15. literally, pluralism, presence, humanism, conservative (pp. 334-335)

PART VII: IN FOCUS—IMPORTANT ISSUES

- Define each of the following *marriage patterns.*

    Endogamy: Exogamy:

    Monogamy: Polygamy:

    Polyandry: Polygyny:

- Define each of the following *residential patterns.*

    Patrilocality: Matrilocality: Neolocality:

- Define *descent* and identify and define the three major types of descent.

- What are the four functions of the family according to *structural-functionalists*?

- What are three ways in which the family perpetuates inequality according to *conflict-theorists*?

- What do proponents of *micro-level analysis* mean by *constructing family life*?

- Describe each of the following *stages of family life* as reviewed in the text.

  Courtship and Romantic Love:

  Settling In:

  Child Rearing:

  The Family in Later Life:

- Identify one major point made about family life relating to each of the following variables.

  Social Class:

  Ethnicity and Race:

  Gender:

- What are the six *cause of divorce* as identified in the text?

- Identify the four *alternative family forms* discussed in the text. List one important demographic fact about each of these forms.

- Define and illustrate each of the following concepts relating to religion.

  Religion:

  Sacred: Profane:

  Ritual: Faith:

- According to *structural-functionalist* Emile Durkheim, what are the basic functions of religion?

- What points are made by *symbolic-interactions,* like Peter Berger, concenring religion?

- How does *conflict theorist* Karl Marx view religion?

- What is Max Weber's point about the relationship between *Protestantism and capitalism*?

- Define each of the following types of *religious organization.*

  Church:

  Denomination: Ecclesia:

  Sect:

  Cult:

- What are the major points being made in the text concerning *religion and social stratification*?

  Social class:

  Ethnicity:

  Race:

- What is *religious fundamentalism*? What are its five *distinctive characteristics*?

PART VIII: COMMENT AND ANALYSIS

Global Sociology

"Early To Wed: A Report From Rural India"

Key Points: Questions:

Controversy and Debate

"Should We Save the Traditional Family?"

Key Points: Questions:

Window on the World--Global Map 12-1

"Marital Form in Global Perspective"

Key Points: Questions:

Seeing Ourselves--National Map 12-1

"Divorced People across the U.S."

Key Points:

Questions:

Controversy and Debate

" Does Science Threaten Religion"

Key Points:

Questions:

Exploring Cyber-Society

"The Cyber-Church: Logging on to Religion"

Key Points:

Questions:

Seeing Ourselves—National Map 12-2

"Religious Diversity across the United States"

Key Points:

Questions:

13 | Education and Medicine

PART I: CHAPTER OUTLINE

X. Theoretical Analysis of Health and Medicine
    A.   Structural-Functional Analysis
    B.   Symbolic-Interaction Analysis
    C.   Social Conflict Analysis
XI.   Looking Ahead: Health in the Twenty-First Century
XII.   Summary
    A.   Education
    B.   Medicine
XIII.   Key Concepts
    A.   Education
    B.   Medicine
XIV.   Critical Thinking Questions
XV.   Learning Exercises

PART II: LEARNING OBJECTIVES

1. To be able to describe the different role of education in low-income and high-income countries.
2. To compare education in India, Japan, and Great Britain to that provided in the United States.
3. To be able to identify and describe the functions of schooling.
4. To consider how education supports social inequality.
5. To be able to discuss the major issues and problems facing contemporary education in the United States today.
6. To be able to identify and evaluate alternatives to the current structure of the institution of education in our society.
7. To become aware of the ways in which the health of a population is shaped by society.
8. To develop a global and historical perspective on health and illness.
9. To recognize how race, social class, and age affect the health of individuals in our society.
10. To be able to discuss cigarette smoking, eating disorders, and sexually transmitted diseases as serious health problems in our society.
11. To be able to recognize and evaluate ethical issues surrounding dying and death.
12. To be able to compare and evaluate the relative effectiveness of scientific medicine and holistic medicine.
13. To be able to compare and evaluate the relative effectiveness of medicine in socialist and capitalists societies.
14. To be able to differentiate between the viewpoints being provided by the three major sociological perspectives.

PART III: KEY CONCEPTS

Education:

A Nation At Risk
charter schools
Coleman Report
credentialism
dropping out
education

functional illiteracy
juku
mainstreaming
mandatory education laws
mass education
political correctness
progressive education
schooling
schooling for profit
silent classroom
student passivity
tracking

Medicine:

AIDS
anorexia nervosa
direct-fee system
euthanasia
health
health care
HIV
HMO
holistic medicine
living will
medicine
physician's role
psychosomatic disorder
scientific medicine
sick role
social epidemiology
socialized medicine
WHO

PART IV: IMPORTANT RESEARCHERS

David Karp and William Yoels   Randall Collins

James Coleman   Jonathan Kozol

Theodore Sizer   Talcott Parsons

Erving Goffman

PART V: STUDY QUESTIONS

True-False--Education

1. T F Today, schooling in *low-income nations* is very diverse because it reflects the local culture.
2. T F The United States actually has a *higher* illiteracy rate than most Latin American societies.
3. T F The United States graduates a *smaller percentage* of its students from high school than does Japan.
4. T F Japan still does not have national *mandatory education laws*.
5. T F The United States was among the first nations to endorse the principle of *mass education*.
6. T F The United States has a *smaller* percentage of its adult population holding a college degree than most other industrialized societies.
7. T F About twenty-five percent of adults in the U.S. have a *college degree*.
8. T F *Social conflict* theorists support *tracking* in that they believe it gives students the kind of learning that fits their abilities and motivation.
9. T F Roughly seventy percent of primary and secondary school children in the U.S. attend *public schools*.
10. T F The *Coleman Report* determined that the amount of educational funding was the most important factor in determining education achievement.
11. T F About sixty-five percent of high-school graduates in the U.S. enroll in college the following fall.
12. T F Male college graduates can expect to earn about forty percent more than female college graduates in their lifetime.
13. T F The argument is being made that an emphasis on *credentialism* in our society leads to a condition of undereducation as people seek the status of a career and its earnings over the completion of degree programs at college.
14. T F Researchers cited in the text found *student passivity* in college to be common, estimating that only about ten percent of class time is spent in discussion.
15. T F The work *A Nation At Risk* focuses on the increasing violence in American schools.
16. T F *Charter schools* refer to schools that operate with less state regulation so teachers and administrators can try new teaching strategies.
17. T F *Mainstreaming* is a form of *inclusive education*.

True-False-Medicine

1. T F The World Health Organization defines *health* as simply the absence of disease.
2. T F The top five *causes of death* in the U.S. have changed very little since 1900.
3. T F Sex is a stronger predictor of health than race.
4. T F *Tobacco* is a 30 billion dollar a year industry in the United States.
5. T F *Eating disorders* have a significant cultural component as evidenced by the fact that 95 percent of people who suffer from anorexia nervosa or bulimia are women, mostly from white, affluent families.
6. T F *Venereal diseases* first emerged on the world scene during the fifteenth century during the European conquest of the Americas.

204

7.	T	F	In 1997, the Supreme Court decided that under the U.S. Constitution, there is no "right to die."
8.	T	F	The *American Medical Association* was founded in 1945.
9.	T	F	*Holistic medicine* stresses that physicians have to take the primary responsibility for health care in society.
10.	T	F	Approximately 70 percent of *physicians* in the new Russian Federation are women.
11.	T	F	The U.S. is unique among industrialized societies in lacking government programs that ensure basic medical care to every citizen.
12.	T	F	Only about 25 percent of the U.S. population has some private or company-paid medical insurance coverage.
13.	T	F	Most surgery in the U.S. is *elective*, or not prompted by a medical emergency.
14.	T	F	One criticism of the *symbolic-interaction* paradigm is that this approach seems to deny that there are any objective standards of well-being.
15.	T	F	The most common objection to the *conflict approach* to the study of health and health care is that it minimizes the advances in U.S. health supported by scientific medicine and higher living standards.

Multiple Choice--Education

1. The extra, intensive schooling received by *Japanese* elementary school children in the afternoon takes place within the:

   (a) quitos.
   (b) huanco.
   (c) taruku.
   (d) mitchou.
   (e) juku.

2. The social institution guiding a society's transmission of knowledge--including basic facts, job skills, and also cultural norms and values--to its members is the definition for:

   (a) schooling.
   (b) teaching.
   (c) education.
   (d) curriculum.

3. *Mandatory education* laws were found in every state in the U.S. by:

   (a) 1781.
   (b) 1850.
   (c) 1822.
   (d) 1918.

4. Which of the following nations has the highest percentage of adults with a *college degree?*

   (a) the United States
   (b) Netherlands
   (c) Canada
   (d) Denmark
   (e) Sweden

5. According to *structural-functionalists*, which of the following functions of formal education helps forge a population into a single, unified society?

   (a) socialization
   (b) social placement
   (c) social integration
   (d) cultural innovation

6. *Structural-functionalists* overlook one core truth:

   (a) education serves as a form of social placement
   (b) the quality of schooling is far greater for some than others
   (c) schools serve several latent functions
   (d) schooling helps forge a mass of people into a unified society
   (e) education creates as well as transmits culture

7. *Social-conflict* analysis associates formal education with:

   (a) student's skill enhancement.
   (b) the improvement of personal well-being.
   (c) patterns of social inequality.
   (d) global competitiveness.

8. *Social conflict analysis* uses the term _____ to refer to the assignment of students to different types of educational programs.

   (a) hierarchial education
   (b) residual education
   (c) ability placement
   (d) competitive placement
   (e) tracking

9. The *Coleman Report* concluded that:

   (a) social inequality is not a problem in public education within our society.
   (b) the simple answer to quality education is more funding for schools.
   (c) minority schools are actually better than schools that are predominately white schools in terms of their student achievement.
   (d) education is the great equalizer, and stressing the importance of differences between families is not particularly important for educational achievement.
   (e) schools alone cannot overcome social inequality.

10. Evaluating people on the basis of *educational degrees* refers to:

   (a) student passivity.
   (b) Tracking.
   (c) Credentialism.
   (d) charter schools.

11. According to Thomas Sizer, rigid expectations, specialization, and rigid conformity are aspects of large bureaucratic schools that:

   (a) undermines education.
   (b) enhance advancement.
   (c) reduce dropout rates.
   (d) improve academic performance.

12. Currently, what percentage of people between the ages of sixteen and twenty-four in the U.S. have *dropped out* of school?

   (a) 5
   (b) 11
   (c) 19
   (d) 25

13. The National Commission on Excellence in Education (1983) issued a report called *A Nation At Risk,* in which it recommended:

   (a) ending student passivity.
   (b) increasing credentialism.
   (c) more stringent educational requirements.
   (d) reducing the length of time students spend in school to allow more students to learn practical skills through employment.

14. *Functional illiteracy* refers to:

   (a) an inability to read and write at all.
   (b) an inability to read at the appropriate level of schooling based on one's age.
   (c) an inability to write.
   (d) reading and writing skills insufficient for everyday living.

15. The *school choice* model focuses on the idea of:

    (a)   competition.
    (b)   consensus.
    (c)   science.
    (d)   integration.

Multiple Choice--Medicine

1. The *health* of any population is shaped by:

    (a)   the society's cultural standards.
    (b)   the society's technology.
    (c)   the society's social inequality.
    (d)   all of the above

2. The *World Health organization* reports that _____ people around the world suffer from serious illness due to poverty.

    (a)   100,000
    (b)   500,000
    (c)   750,000
    (d)   1 billion
    (e)   2.5 billion

3. During the first half of the nineteenth century in Europe and the United States, the improvement in health was primarily due to:

    (a)   the rising standard of living.
    (b)   medical advances.
    (c)   changes in cultural values toward medicine.
    (d)   immigration.

4. In 1900, _____ caused one-fourth of deaths in the U.S. Today, however, most deaths are caused by:

    (a)   chronic diseases, infectious diseases.
    (b)   accidents, crime.
    (c)   infectious diseases, chronic diseases.
    (d)   cancer, accidents.
    (e)   crime, accidents.

5. _____ is the study of how health and disease are distributed throughout a society's population.

   (a) Demography
   (b) Social epidemiology
   (c) Epistomolgy
   (d) Medicationalization

6. Which of the following is *true* concerning age, sex, and health in the United States?

   (a) Across the life course, men are healthier than women.
   (b) Males have a slight biological advantage that renders them less likely than females to die before or immediately after birth.
   (c) Socialization aids men's health to a greater degree than it does women's health.
   (d) Young women are more likely to die than young men.
   (e) Across the life course, women are healthier than men.

7. Which of the following were the *leading causes of death* in the U.S. in 1900?

   (a) accidents and heart disease
   (b) cancer and diphtheria
   (c) influenza and pneumonia
   (d) lung disease and kidney disease
   (e) homicide and diabetes

8. *Life expectancy for African Americans is _____ years less than for whites.*

   (a) 10
   (b) 2
   (c) 9
   (d) 6
   (e) 12

9. According to medical experts, about how many people die in the U.S. each year as a direct result of *smoking*?

   (a) 100,000
   (b) 50,000
   (c) 200,000
   (d) 1 million
   (e) 450,000

10. Of the reported cases of *gonorrhea* and *syphilis* in the U.S., the vast majority involved:

    (a)   whites.
    (b)   African Americans.
    (c)   Hispanics.
    (d)   Asians.

11. In 1997, the total number of people in the U.S. would have been diagnosed with HIV was:

    (a)   100,000.
    (b)   600,000.
    (c)   900,000.
    (d)   1,700,000.

12. The institutionalization of *scientific medicine* by the AMA resulted in:

    (a)   expensive medical education.
    (b)   domination of medicine by white males.
    (c)   an inadequate supply of physicians in rural areas.
    (d)   all of the above

13. *Holistic medicine* is a reaction to scientific medicine. Which of the following is *not* an emphasis advocates of holistic medicine share?

    (a)   an emphasis upon the environment in which the person exists
    (b)   an emphasis upon the responsibility of society for health promotion and care
    (c)   an emphasis upon optimum health for all
    (d)   an emphasis upon the home setting for medical treatment

14. *European* governments pay about _____ percent of medical costs, whereas in the *United States*, the government pays about _____ percent of medical costs.

    (a)   80/44
    (b)   100/10
    (c)   25/50
    (d)   40/60

15. Which country does not offer a comprehensive health program to the entire population?

    (a)   Sweden
    (b)   Great Britain
    (c)   the United States
    (d)   Canada

16. _____ refers to a health-care system in which the government owns and operates most medical facilities and employs most physicians.

    (a) A health maintenance organization
    (b) Socialized medicine
    (c) A direct-fee system
    (d) Holistic medicine

17. An association that provides comprehensive medical care for a fixed fee is termed a(n):

    (a) WHO.
    (b) DFS.
    (c) AMA.
    (d) HMO.

18. Which of the following *theoretical paradigms* in sociology utilizes concepts like *sick role* and *physician's role* to help explain health behavior?

    (a) social-conflict
    (b) social-exchange
    (c) symbolic-interaction
    (d) structural-functional
    (e) materialism

19. Which of the following *theoretical paradigms* in sociology focuses on the issues of *access* and *profits* in the study of health care?

    (a) social-conflict
    (b) structural-functional
    (c) symbolic-interaction
    (d) social-exchange

20. What percentage of surgical operations in the U.S. each year are *elective*?

    (a) one-fifth
    (b) one-fourth
    (c) one-half
    (d) three-quarters

Matching--Education

1. ____ Evaluating people on the basis of education degrees.
2. ____ A 1983 study on the quality of schooling.
3. ____ The assignment of students to different types of educational programs.

211

4.   ___   The percentage of high-school graduates who attend college the same year as receiving their high-school diploma.

5.   ___   The percentage of the 55 million primary and secondary school children attending state-funded public schools.

6.   ___   The percentage of students bused outside their neighborhoods.

7.   ___   Schooling in the U.S. reflects the value of _____.

8.   ___   The percentage of U.S. adults aged 25-64 with a college degree.

9.   ___   Confirmed that predominately minority schools suffer problems, but cautioned that money alone will not magically improve academic quality.

10.   ___   Argues that tracking is one of the "savage inequalities" in our school system.

a.	tracking	f.	5
b.	65	g.	James Coleman
c.	equal opportunity	h.	Jonathan Kozol
d.	credentiaism	i.	A Nation at Risk
e.	25	j.	86

Matching--Medicine

1.   ___   The number one cause of death in the U.S. today.

2.   ___   The study of how health and disease are distributed throughout a society's population.

3.   ___   An approach to health care that emphasizes prevention of illness and takes account of the person's entire physical and social environment.

4.   ___   The social institution that focuses on combating disease and improving health.

5.   ___   A medical-care system in which the government owns most facilities and employs most physicians.

6.   ___   The percentage of health expenditures paid by the government in the U.S. today.

7.   ___   Patterns of behavior defined as appropriate for those who are ill.

8.   ___   The number two cause of death in the U.S. today.

9.   ___   Percentage of physicians in Russia who are women.

10.   ___   The percentage of health expenditures paid by European governments today.

a.	sick role	f.	80
b.	cancer	g.	medicine
c.	socialized medicine	h.	heart disease
d.	70	i.	44
e.	social epidemiology	j.	holistic medicine

Fill-In--Education

1. The social institution through which society provides its members with important knowledge, including basic facts, job skills, and cultural values and norms is termed _____.

2. In Japan, because of competitive exams, only _____ *percent* of high school graduates enter college.

3. By _____ all of the states in the U.S. had *mandatory education laws.*

4. Schooling in the U.S. reflects our *cultural values* of _____ and _____ learning.

5. The assignment of students to different types of educational programs is referred to as _____.

6. Although only _____ percent of U.S. school children are *bused to schools outside their neighborhoods for racial balance purposes*, this policy has generated heated controversy.

7. The *Coleman Report* suggests that even if school funding were exactly the same everywhere, students whose _____ value and encourage education would still perform better.

8. The most crucial factor affecting access to U.S. higher education is _____.

9. The average *annual earnings* for a male with a high-school education is about $ _____, while the average earnings for a woman with a college education is about $ _____.

10. _____ is evaluating a person on the basis of educational degrees.

11. *Theodore Sizer* identified through his research five ways in which large, _____ schools undermine education, including rigid conformity, numerical rating, rigid expectations, specialization, and little individual responsibility.

12. The 1983 report by the National Commission on Excellence in Education was entitled _____.

13. _____ _____ refers to the integrating of special students into the overall educational program.

14. Three alternative approaches to increasing *school choice* include giving _____ to families with school-aged children and allow them to spent that money on any school they want, _____ for profit, and _____ schools.

15. About _____ million adults in the U.S. are now enrolled in college.

Fill-In--Medicine

1. Society shapes the *health* of people in five major ways. These include: People judge their health in relations to _____ they know, people define as "healthy" what they think of as _____ good, cultural _____ of health change over time, health relates to a society's _____, health relates to social _____.

2. After 1850, *medical advances* began to improve health, primarily by controlling _____ diseases.

3. In 1900, _____ and _____ caused one-fourth of all *deaths* in the United States.

4. *Social* _____ is the study of how health and disease are distributed throughout a society's population.

5. The leading cause of death today in the U.S. is _____.

6. Death is now rare among young people, with two notable exceptions: a rise in mortality resulting from _____ and, more recently, from _____.

7. Consumption of *cigarettes* has fallen since 1960, when almost _____ percent of U.S. adults smoked. Today, only about _____ percent of U.S. adults are smokers.

8. _____ percent of people who suffer from *anorexia nervosa* or *bulimia* are women.

9. AIDS, acquired immune deficiency syndrome, is caused by _____, or the human immunodeficiency virus.

10. *HIV* is *infectious* but not _____.

11. Specific behaviors put people at high risk for *HIV* infection. These include _____ sex, sharing _____, and using any kind of _____.

12. _____ is assisting in the death of a person suffering from an incurable disease.

13. *Holistic medicine* favors _____ rather than a _____ approach to illness.

14. _____ *medicine* is an approach to health care that emphasizes prevention of illness and takes account of the person's entire physical and social environment.

15. About _____ percent of U.S. physicians are *women*.

16. While *European* governments pay for about eighty percent of their people's medical costs, in the *United States* the government pays for about _____ percent.

17. Expenditures for medical care in the United States has increased dramatically since 1950. The medical care bill of the U.S. in 1996 was over _____ *dollars* or about _____ *dollars* per person.

18. The _____ _____ refers to patterns of behavior defined as appropriate for those who are ill.

19. One strength of the _____ *paradigm* lies in revealing that what people view as healthful or harmful depends on numerous factors, many of which are not, strictly speaking, medical.

20. *Social-conflict* analysis focuses attention on the _____ issue, the _____ motive, and medicine as _____ in helping us understand health and medical care in our society.

Definition and Short-Answer

1. Describe the four basic *functions* of education as reviewed in the text.
2. What were the basic findings of the *Coleman Report*?
3. How do *annual earnings* differ for men and women given the same levels of education achievement?
4. What are the five serious problems with the *bureaucratic* nature of our educational system?
5. What recommendations were made in the report *A Nation At Risk*?
6. Differentiate between the educational systems of the U.S., India, Great Britain, and Japan.
7. What are the major *problems* in U.S. education? Identify the specific factors involved in each problem identified. What is one recommendation you have to solving each of the problems?
8. What are the three alternative approaches identified as ways of increasing *school choice*? What are your opinions on each of these?
9. It is pointed out in the text that the *health* of any population is shaped by important characteristics of the society as a whole. What are three general characteristics and an example of each?
10. How have the *causes of death* changed in the U.S. over the last century?
11. What is *social epidemiology*? Provide two illustrations of patterns of health found using this approach.
12. What is *AIDS*? How is it transmitted?
13. What is meant by the *sick role*?
14. Describe the three basic characteristics of *holistic medicine*.
15. In what ways does the health-care system of the U.S. differ from health-care systems in other capitalist systems?

16. What are *social-conflict* analysts' arguments about the health care system in the United States?
17. What factors are identified as reasons for why the U.S. does not have a *national health-care system*?
18. What do *symbolic-interactionists* mean by *socially constructing illness* and *socially constructing treatment*?

PART VI: ANSWERS TO STUDY QUESTIONS

True-False--Education

1.	T	(p. 343)	11.	F	(p. 347)
2.	F	(p. 342)	12.	F	(p. 348)
3.	T	(pp. 343-344)	13.	T	(p. 348)
4.	F	(p. 344)	14.	T	(p. 350)
5.	T	(p. 343)	15.	F	(p. 351)
6.	F	(p. 344)	16.	T	(p. 352)
7.	T	(p. 344)	17.	T	(p. 352)
8.	F	(p. 345)			
9.	F	(p. 346)			
10.	F	(p. 347)			

True-False--Medicine

1.	F	(p. 354)	9.	F	(p. 363)
2.	F	(p. 355)	10.	T	(p. 364)
3.	T	(p. 357)	11.	T	(p. 365)
4.	T	(p. 357)	12.	F	(p. 365)
5.	T	(p. 358)	13.	T	(p. 367)
6.	T	(p. 358)	14.	T	(p. 367)
7.	T	(p. 358)	15.	T	(p. 368)
8.	F	(p. 361)			

Multiple Choice--Education

1.	e	(p. 341)	9.	c	(p. 347)
2.	c	(p. 341)	10.	c	(p. 348)
3.	d	(p. 343)	11.	a	(p. 349)
4.	a	(p. 344)	12.	b	(p. 350)
5.	c	(p. 344)	13.	c	(p. 351)
6.	b	(p. 345)	14.	d	(p. 351)
7.	c	(p. 345)	15.	a	(p. 352)
8.	e	(p. 345)			

Multiple Choice--Medicine

1.	d	(p. 354)	11.	b	(p. 359)
2.	d	(p. 355)	12.	d	(pp. 362-363)
3.	a	(p. 355)	13.	b	(p. 363)
4.	c	(p. 355)	14.	a	(p. 365)
5.	b	(p. 356)	15.	c	(p. 365)
6.	e	(pp. 356-357)	16.	b	(p. 364)
7.	c	(p. 355)	17.	d	(p. 365)
8.	d	(p. 357)	18.	d	(p. 366)
9.	e	(p. 357)	19.	a	(p. 367)
10.	b	(p. 358)	20.	d	(p. 367)

Matching--Education

1.	d	(p. 348)	6.	f	(p. 347)
2.	i	(p. 346)	7.	c	(p. 344)
3.	a	(p. 345)	8.	e	(p. 344)
4.	b	(p. 347)	9.	g	(p. 347)
5.	j	(p. 346)	10.	h	(p. 346)

Matching-Medicine

1.	h	(p. 355)	6.	i	(p. 365)
2.	e	(p. 356)	7.	a	(p. 366)
3.	j	(p. 365)	8.	b	(p. 355)
4.	g	(p. 354)	9.	d	(p. 364)
5.	c	(p. 364)	10.	f	(p. 365)

Fill-In--Education

1.	education (p. 341)	9.	$31,215, $35,379 (p. 348)
2.	30 (pp. 343-344)	10.	Credentialism (p. 348)
3.	1918 (p. 343)	11.	bureaucratic (p. 349)
4.	equal, practical (p. 344)	12.	A Nation at Risk (p. 351)
5.	tracking (p. 345)	13.	mainstreaming (p. 353)
6.	5 (p. 347)	14.	vouchers, profit, charter (p. 352)
7.	families (p. 347)	15.	25 (p. 353
8.	money (p. 347)		

1.   cultural, morally, standards, technology, inequality (p. 354)
2.   infectious (p. 355)
3.   influenza, pneumonia (p. 355)
4.   epidemiology (p. 356)
5.   heart disease (p. 355)
6.   accidents, AIDS (p. 356)
7.   45, 25 (p. 357)
8.   95 (p. 358)
9.   HIV (p. 359)
10.   contagious (p. 359)
11.   anal, needles, drugs (p. 361)
12.   Euthanasia (p. 361)
13.   active, reactive (p.363)
14.   Holistic (p.363)
15.   26 (p. 364)
16.   80, 44 (p. 365)
17.   trillion, 3,300 (p. 365)
18.   sick role (p. 366)
19.   symbolic-interaction (p. 366)
20.   access, profit, politics (pp. 367-368)

PART VII: IN FOCUS—IMPORTANT ISSUES

- Describe schooling in *low-income countries* using India to illustrate.

- Describe schooling in *high-income countries* using Japan to illustrate.

- What two *cultural values* are reflected in U.S. education?

- According to *structural-functionalists*, what are the five ways in which schooling enhances the operation and stability of society?

What do critics of structural-functionalism argue about this perspective view of schooling?

- According to *social-conflict theorists*, what are three ways in which schooling causes and perpetuates social inequality?

- Provide evidence for each of the following *problems in U.S. education*.

  Discipline and Violence:

  Bureaucracy and Student Passivity:

  College: The Silent Classroom:

  Dropping Out:

  Academic Standards:

- Discuss each of the following *recent issues in U.S. education*.

  School Choice:

  Schooling People with Disabilities:

  Adult Education:

- Identify and describe the three major ways *society affects health*:

- Describe the general health conditions for the following categories of nations.

  Low-income countries:

  High-income countries:

- Identify two important points made in the text concerning each of the following health issues.

  Cigarette Smoking:

  Eating Disorders:

  Sexually Transmitted Disorders:

- Do people have a *right to die*? What do you think?

- How is medicine *paid for* in the following countries?

  The People's Republic of China:

  The Russian Federation:

  Sweden:

  Great Britain:

  Canada:

  Japan:

  The United States:

- How does each of the following *theoretical paradigms* help us understand health and medicine in our society?

  Structural-Functionalism:

  Social-Conflict Theory:

  Symbolic-Interactionism:

PART VIII: ANALYSIS AND COMMENT

Sociology of Everyday Life

"Masculinity: A Threat to Health?"

Key Points: Questions:

Controversy and Debate

"The Genetic Crystal Ball: Do We Really Want to Look?"

Key Points: Questions:

Seeing Ourselves--National Map 13-1

"College Attendance across the United States"

Key Points: Questions:

Window on the World--Global Maps 13 –1 and 13-2

"Illiteracy in Global Perspective"

Key Points: Questions:

"HIV Infection of Adults in Global Perspective"

Key Points: Questions:

14 Population And Urbanization

PART I: CHAPTER OUTLINE

I.   Demography: The Study of Population
    A.   Fertility
    B.   Mortality
    C.   Migration
    D.   Population Growth
    E.   Population Composition

II.   History and Theory of Population Growth
    A.   Malthusian Theory
    B.   Demographic Transition Theory

III. Global Population: A Survey
    A.   The Low-Growth North
    B.   The High-Growth South

IV.   Urbanization: The Growth of Cities
    A.   The Evolution of Cities
    B.   The Growth of U.S. Cities
    C.   Suburbs and Urban Decline
    D.   Postindustrial Sunbelt Cities
    E.   Megalopolis: Regional Cities
    F.   Edge Cities

IV.   Urbanization As A Way of Life
    A.   Ferdinand Tonnies: Gemeinschaft and Gesellschaft
    B.   Emile Durkheim: Mechanical and Organic Solidarity
    C.   Georg Simmel: The Blase' Urbanite
    D.   The Chicago School: Robert Park and Louis Wirth
    E.   Urban Ecology
    F.   Urban Political Economy

V.   Urbanization In Poor Societies
    A.   Looking Ahead: Population and Urbanization in the Twenty-First Century

VI.   Summary
VII. Key Concepts
VIII. Critical-Thinking Questions
IX.   Learning Exercises

PART II: LEARNING OBJECTIVES

1. To learn the basic concepts used by demographers to study populations.
2. To be able to compare Malthusian theory and demographic transition theory.
3. To be able to recognize how populations differ in industrial and nonindustrial societies.
4. To gain an understanding of the worldwide urbanization process, and to be able to put it into historical perspective.
5. To be able to describe demographic changes in the U.S. throughout its history.
6. To consider urbanism as a way of life as viewed by several historical figures in sociology.
7. To consider the idea of urban ecology.

PART III: KEY CONCEPTS

Population:

age-sex pyramid
crude birth rate
crude death rate
demographic transition theory
demography
doubling time
emigration
fecundity
fertility
immigration
infant mortality rate
life expectancy
Maltusian theory
migration
mortality
natural growth rate
net-migration
sex ratio
zero population growth

Urbanization:

edge city
Gemeinschaft
Gesellscaft
megalopolis

suburbs
urbanization
urban ecology
urban renewal

PART IV: IMPORTANT RESEARCHERS

Ferdinand Tonnies   Emile Durkheim

Robert Park   Louis Wirth

Georg Simmel   Thomas Malthus

PART V: STUDY QUESTIONS

True-False

1.	T	F	*Demography* refers to the study of human population.
2.	T	F	Demographers using what is known as the *crude birth rate* only take into account women of childbearing age in the calculation of population growth.
3.	T	F	In general, population is moving from the *coasts* to the *heartland* in the United States.
4.	T	F	*Emigration* is measured in terms of the *out-migration rate*, or the number leaving for every thousand people.
5.	T	F	The U.S., using the demographer's *natural growth rate* measure, is experiencing a significant decline in population.
6.	T	F	A handy rule-of-thumb for estimating population growth is dividing a society's growth rate into seventy to calculate the *doubling time* in years. Thus, an annual growth rate of 2 percent doubles a population in thirty-five years.

7.	T	F	A significantly larger percentage of the U.S. population over the next two decades will be comprised of *childbearing aged females* that at any other period in our nation's history.
8.	T	F	The world's population reached 1 billion in 1800, 2 billion in 1930, 3 billion in 1963, 4 billion in 1974, 5 billion in 1987, and 6 billion in 2000.
9.	T	F	*Malthusian theory* predicted that while population would increase in a *geometric progression*, food supplies would increase only by an *arithmetic progression*.
10.	T	F	*Demographic transition theory* suggests the key to population control lies in *technology*.
11.	T	F	In poor countries through the world, birth rates have *fallen* since 1950.
12.	T	F	Poor societies now account for two-thirds of all the earth's people and 90 percent of global population increase.
13.	T	F	The *first urban revolution* occurred about 500 years ago.
14.	T	F	Urbanization began in *Europe* in about 1800 B.C.E.
15.	T	F	By about 1750, the *Industrial Revolution* triggered a *second urban revolution*.
16.	T	F	Most of the ten *largest cities in the U.S.* (by population) are in the *Sunbelt*.
17.	T	F	A *megalopolis* is also known as a regional city.
18.	T	F	Compared to Louis Wirth, Robert Park had a relatively negative view of *urban life*.
19.	T	F	The *third urban revolution* began around 1950 and continues to this day.
20.	T	F	The population growth of urban areas in poor societies located in Latin America, Asia, and Africa is *twice* the rate for their societies as a whole.

Multiple-Choice

1. How many people are added to the planet *each year*?

    (a) 5 million
    (b) 20 million
    (c) 1 billion
    (d) 78 million

2. In 1999 the world population stood at approximately:

    (a) 2 billion.
    (b) 4 billion.
    (c) 6 billion.
    (d) 8 billion.

3. The incidence of childbearing in a society's population refers to:

    (a) fertility.
    (b) fecundity.
    (c) demography.
    (d) the sex ratio.
    (e) life expectancy.

4. *Fecundity* is sharply reduced in practice by:

   (a)   cultural norms.
   (b)   finances.
   (c)   personal choice.
   (d)   all of the above

5. Which region of the world has the *highest* birth rate, death rate, and infant mortality rate?

   (a)   Latin America
   (b)   Asia
   (c)   Europe
   (d)   Oceania
   (e)   Africa

6. The movement of people into and out of a specified territory is:

   (a)   demographic transition.
   (b)   migration.
   (c)   fecundity.
   (d)   mortality.
   (e)   fertility.

7. In 1998, the *sex-ratio* in the U.S. was:

   (a)   85.
   (b)   100.
   (c)   90.
   (d)   105.
   (e)   96.

8. During the twentieth century, the world's population has increased _____ *-fold*.

   (a)   two
   (b)   three
   (c)   four
   (d)   five
   (e)   six

9. *Demographic transition theory* links population patterns to a society's:

   (a)   religious beliefs and practices.
   (b)   technological development.
   (c)   natural resources.
   (d)   sexual norms.

10. *Stage 3* of the demographic transition theory is characterized by:

    (a)   increasing death rates.
    (b)   increasing birth rates.
    (c)   decreasing death rates.
    (d)   none of the above

11. The *first city* to have ever existed is argued to be:

    (a)   Athens.
    (b)   Cairo.
    (c)   Tikal.
    (d)   Jericho.
    (e)   Rome.

12. *Urbanization in Europe* began about:

    (a)   1800 B.C.E.
    (b)   100 C.E.
    (c)   500 C.E..
    (d)   1800 C.E.

13. According to the text, the *second urban revolution* was triggered by:

    (a)   the fall of Rome.
    (b)   the post-World War II baby boom.
    (c)   the Industrial Revolution.
    (d)   the discovery of the New World.
    (e)   the fall of Greece.

14. The period called the *era of the metropolis* occurred between:

    (a)   1624-1800.
    (b)   1860-1950.
    (c)   1950-1970.
    (d)   1970-present.

15. The period of *1950 to the present* is described in the text as:

    (a)   urban decentralization.
    (b)   the metropolitan era.
    (c)   urban expansion.
    (d)   the second urban revolution.

16. A vast urban region containing a number of cities and their surrounding suburbs is known as a:

    (a) metropolis.
    (b) Suburb.
    (c) Gemeinschaft.
    (d) Megalopolis.

17. *Ferdinand Tonnies'* concept referring to the type of social organization by which people stand apart based on self-interest is:

    (a) megalopolis.
    (b) sector model.
    (c) multi-nuclei model.
    (d) Gemeinschaft.

18. *Emile Durkheim* believed urbanization erodes social bonds based on common sentiments and shared moral values, but also generates:

    (a) organic solidarity.
    (b) chaos.
    (c) a megalopolis.
    (d) Gemienschaft.

19. The link between the *physical* and *social* dimensions of cities is known as:

    (a) Gesellschaft.
    (b) urban ecology.
    (c) organic solidarity.
    (d) Gemeinshcaft.

20. Blending the ideas of Tonnies, Simmel, and Park, this researcher viewed the city as impersonal and superficial. He believed city people notice others not in terms *who* they are but *what* they are.

    (a) Emile Durkheim
    (b) Karl Marx
    (c) Louis Wirth
    (d) Jean Lenski

21. _____ *analysis* is a branch of urban ecology that investigates what people in a particular neighborhood have in common.

    (a) Wedge-shaped
    (b) Concentric zones
    (c) Multicentered model
    (d) Social area

228

22. The *urban political economy model* is influenced by the thinking of:

    (a)   Louis Wirth.
    (b)   Max Weber.
    (c)   Karl Marx.
    (d)   Emile Durkheim.
    (e)   Robert Park.

23. Which of the following is expected to be the *largest urban area* (by population) in the year 2015?

    (a)   Tokyo-Yokohama
    (b)   Shanghai
    (c)   New York
    (d)   Buenos Aires
    (e)   Mexico City

Matching

1. _____ Saw the city as a living organism, truly a human kaleidoscope.
2. _____ Developed the concepts Gemeinschaft and Gesellschaft.
3. _____ Developed the concepts of mechanical and organic solidarity.
4. _____ 1860-1950.
5. _____ Maximum possible childbearing.
6. _____ A type of social organization by which people stand apart from one another in pursuit of self-interest.
7. _____ A theory claiming that population would soon rise out of control.
8. _____ Social bonds based on collective conformity to tradition.
9. _____ Argued that urbanites develop a blasé attitude, selectively tuning out much of what goes on around them.
10. _____ The incidence of childbearing in a society's population.
11. _____ The concentration of humanity into cities
12. _____ A thesis linking population patterns to a society's lvel of technological development.
13. _____ Created by urban decentralization, they are business centers that stand some distance from the old downtowns.
14. _____ The movement of people into and out of a specific territory.

a. Ferdinand Tonnies
b. mechanical solidarity
c. fertility
d. Gesellschaft
e. demographic transition theory
f. metropolis era
g. Robert Park
h. Malthusian theory
i. Emile Durkheim
j. fecundity
k. urbanization
l. Gerg Simmel
m. edge cities
n. Colonial settlement
o. migration

1. _____ refers to the incidence of childbearing in a society's population.
2. _____ refers to the incidence of death in a country's population.
3. The *Crude death rate* in Africa in 1998 was _____.
4. Movement out of a territory—or _____--is measured in terms of an *out-migration rate*.
5. The _____ _____ refers to the number of males for every 100 females in a nation's population.
6. *Thomas Malthus* saw population increasing according to a _____ progression, and food production increasing in an _____ progression.
7. _____ *theory* is the thesis that population patterns are linked to a society's level of technological development.
8. The three factors that set the stage for the development of the first cities were a *favorable* _____, an *advanced* _____, and a *material* _____.
9. The term _____ is from the Greek meaning "mother city."
10. The Bureau of the Census recognizes 256 urban areas in the United States that they call *MSAs*, or _____.
11. _____ refers to a type of social organization by which people are bound closely together by kinship and tradition.
12. _____ _____ is the study of the link between the physical and social dimensions of cities.
13. By 1995, _____ cities had more than 5 million residents, and _____ were in *poor societies*.
14. Throughout history, _____ have *improved* people's standard of living more than any other settlement pattern.

Definition and Short-Answer

1. What are the three basic factors that determine the *size* and *growth rate* of a population? Define each of these concepts.
2. Differentiate between *Malthusian theory* and *demographic transition theory* as perspectives on population growth.
3. Identify and describe the three stages in the *demographic transition theory*.
4. Identify and describe the three *urban revolutions*.
5. Identify and describe the four *periods of growth* in U.S. cities
6. What is *urban ecology? What are two criticisms of this approach?*
7. Discuss significant points made in the text concerning the *high-growth south* and *low-growth north*.
8. What shifts in population have occurred between the S*nowbelt* and *Sunbelt* between1940 and 1998?
9. Identify a U.S. *megalopolis*.

PART VI: ANSWERS TO STUDY QUESTIONS

True-False

1.	T	(p. 375)
2.	F	(p. 376)
3.	F	(p. 377)
4.	T	(p. 377)
5.	F	(p. 378)
6.	T	(p. 379)
7.	F	(p. 379)
8.	T	(p. 380)
9.	T	(p. 380)
10.	T	(p. 381)
11.	T	(p. 382)
12.	T	(p. 382)
13.	F	(p. 384)
14.	T	(p. 384)
15.	T	(p. 385)
16.	T	(p. 388)
17.	T	(p. 388)
18.	F	(pp. 390-391)
19.	T	(p. 393)
20.	T	(p. 393)

Multiple-Choice

1.	d	(p. 375)
2.	c	(p. 375)
3.	a	(p. 376)
4.	d	(p. 376)
5.	e	(p. 376)
6.	b	(p. 377)
7.	e	(p. 379)
8.	c	(p. 380)
9.	b	(p. 381)
10.	c	(p. 381)
11.	d	(p. 384)
12.	a	(p. 384)
13.	c	(p. 385)
14.	b	(p. 387)
15.	a	(p. 387)
16.	d	(p. 388)
17.	d	(p. 389)
18.	a	(p. 390)
19.	b	(p. 391)
20.	c	(p. 391)
21.	d	(p. 391)
22.	c	(p. 393)
23.	a	(p. 394)

Matching

1.	g	(p. 391)
2.	a	(p. 389)
3.	i	(pp. 389-390)
4.	f	(p. 387)
5.	j	(p. 376)
6.	d	(p. 389)
7.	h	(p. 380)
8.	b	(pp. 389-390)
9.	l	(p. 390)
10.	c	(p. 376)
11.	k	(p. 384)
12.	e	(p. 381)
13.	m	(p. 389)
14.	o	(p. 377)

Fill-In

1. Fertility (p. 376)
2. Mortality (p. 376)
3. 14.4 (p. 376)
8. ecology, technology, surplus (p. 384)
9. metropolis (p. 387)
10. metropolitan statistical areas (p. 388)

PART VII: IN FOCUS—IMPORTANT ISSUES

- Define the following *demographic concepts*.

  Fertility:

  Mortality:

  Migration:

- Briefly describe *Malthusian theory*.

- Briefly describe *demographic transition theory*.

- Write a description for each of the following concerning the *evolution of cities*.

  Preconditions of cities:

  The first cities:

  Preindustrial European cities:

  Industrial European cities:

- Briefly describe each of the following stages in the *growth of U.S. cities.*

  Colonial settlement (1624-1800)

  Urban expansion (1800-1860)

  The metropolitan era (1860-1950)

  Urban decentralization (1950-present)

- Identify the major views of *urbanization* for each of the following researchers.

  Ferdinand Tonnies:

  Emile Durkheim:

  Georg Simmel:

  Robert Park:

  Louis Wirth:

PART VIII: COMMENT AND ANALYSIS

Global Sociology

"Empowering Women: The Key to Controlling Population Growth"

Key Points: Questions:

Controversy and Debate

"Apocalypse Soon? Will People Overwhelm the Earth?"

Key Points: Questions:

Window on the World—Global Maps 14-1 and 14-2

"Population Growth in Global Perspective"

Key Points: Questions:

"Urbanization in Global Perspective"

Key Points: Questions:

Seeing Ourselves—National Map 14-1

"Population Change across the United States"

Key Points: Questions:

15 Environment And Society

PART I: CHAPTER OUTLINE

I. Ecology: The Study of the Natural Environment
    A.   The Role of Sociology
    B.   The Global Dimension
    C.   The Historical Dimension
    D.   Population Increase
    E.   Cultural Patterns: Growth and Limits
II. Environmental Issues
    A.   Solid Waste: The "Disposable Society"
    B.   Preserving Clean Water
    C.   Clearing the Air
    D.   Acid Rain
    E.   The Rain Forests
III. Society and the Environment: Theoretical Analysis
    A.   Structural-Functional Analysis
    B.   Cultural Ecology
    C.   Social-Conflict Analysis
    D.   Environmental Racism
IV. Looking Ahead: Toward a Sustainable Society and World
V. Summary
VI. Key Concepts
VII. Critical-Thinking Questions
VIII. Learning Exercises

PART II: LEARNING OBJECTIVES

1. To gain an appreciation for the global dimension of the natural environment.
2. To develop an understanding of how sociology can help us confront environmental issues.
3. To be able to discuss the dimensions of the "logic of growth" and the "limits to growth" as issues and realities confronting our world.
4. To be able to identify and discuss major environmental issues confronting our world today.

5. To be able to identify and discuss the three contrasting theories concerning the relationship between society and the environment.

6. To begin to develop a sense about the ingredients for a sustainable society and world in the century to come.

PART IV: KEY CONCEPTS

acid rain
biodiversity
cultural ecology
disposable society
ecologically sustainable culture
ecology
environmental deficit
environmental racism
greenhouse effect
natural environment
rain forest
recycling

PART V: IMPORTANT RESEARCHERS

Marvin Harris

PART VI: STUDY QUESTIONS

True-False

1.	T	F	The *natural environment* includes the air, water, and soil, but not living organisms.
2.	T	F	About 78 million people are added to the world's population each year.
3.	T	F	The cultural values of material comfort, progress, and science form the foundation for the *logic of growth* thesis.
4.	T	F	The *limits of growth* thesis, stated simply, is that humanity must implement policies to restrain the growth of population, cut back on production, and use fewer natural resources in order to head off environmental collapse.
5.	T	F	The limits to growth theorists are also referred to as *neo-Malthusians*.
6.	T	F	The United States is being characterized in the text as a *disposable society*.
7.	T	F	Almost one-half of all household trash in the U.S. is composed of plastic, glass, and food waste.
8.	T	F	Over one-half of all *solid waste* in the U.S. is burned or recycled.

9.	T	F	According to what scientists call the *hydological cycle*, the earth naturally recycles water and refreshes the land.
10.	T	F	Households around the world account for more *water use* than does industry.
11.	T	F	*Biodiversity* tends to be relatively low in rain forest environments.
12.	T	F	The *greenhouse effect* is the result of too little carbon dioxide in the atmosphere.
13.	T	F	One criticism of the *structural-functional* paradigm is that it fails to take account of the interconnectedness of various dimensions of social life.
14.	T	F	According to *social-conflict* theorists, rich nations are overdeveloped and consume too much of the world's natural resources.

Multiple Choice

1. _____ is the study of the interaction of living organisms and the natural environment.

    (a) Environmentalism
    (b) Sociobiology
    (c) Ecosystem
    (d) Ecology

2. The Greek meaning of the word *eco* is:

    (a) weather .
    (b) satisfaction.
    (c) house.
    (d) work.
    (e) material.

2. _____ is a system composed of the interaction of all living organisms and their natural environment.

    (a) Ecosystem
    (b) Environment
    (c) Biosphere
    (d) Ecology

4. Riddle: A pond has a single water lily growing on it. The lily doubles in size each day, In thirty days, it covers the entire pond. On which day did it cover half the pond?

    (a) 5
    (b) 21
    (c) 8
    (d) 15
    (e) 29

5.   By the year 2050, the *world's population* is expected to reach:

    (a)   4 billion.
    (b)   6 billion.
    (c)   8 billion.
    (d)   11 billion.

6.   Which of the following cultural values form the foundation of the *logic of growth* perspective?

    (a)   material comfort
    (b)   progress
    (c)   science
    (d)   all of the above
    (e)   none of the above

7.   Which of the following is *not* a projection for the twenty-first century using the *limits of growth thesis*?

    (a)   a stabilizing, then declining population
    (b)   declining industrial output per capita
    (c)   increasing, then declining pollution
    (d)   increasing food per capita

8.   How many pounds of *solid waste* are generated in the U.S. each day?

    (a)   15 million
    (b)   1 billion
    (c)   100 million
    (d)   8 billion
    (e)   250 million

8.   Which type of solid waste represents about *one-half* of all household trash in the U.S.?

    (a)   metal products
    (b)   yard waste
    (c)   paper
    (d)   plastic
    (e)   glass

10.   What percentage of the solid waste in the U.S. is *recycled*?

    (a)   2
    (b)   30
    (c)   10
    (d)   60
    (e)   5

12. *Rain forests* cover approximately _____ percent of the earth's land surface.

   (a)   0.01
   (b)   7
   (c)   2
   (d)   11
   (e)   20

13. The world's *largest rain forest* is found in:

   (a)   South America
   (b)   Indonesia.
   (c)   Africa.
   (d)   Asia.

14. *Rain forests* are home to almost _____ percent of our planet's species.

   (a)   90
   (b)   75
   (c)   50
   (d)   30

15. The *structural-functional* paradigm offers three important insights about the natural environment. These include:

   (a)   the importance of values and beliefs to the operation of a social system
   (b)   the interconnectedness of various dimensions of social life
   (c)   some strategies for responding to environmental problems
   (d)   all of the above

16. Strategies recommended for creating a sustainable ecosystem include:

   (a)   conservation.
   (b)   bringing population under control.
   (c)   reducing waste.
   (d)   all of the above

17. A collection of environmental strategies alone will not succeed without some fundamental changes in the ways in which we think about ourselves and our world. Important points to consider include:

   (a)   the present is tied to the future
   (b)   humans are linked in countless ways to all other species of life
   (c)   achieving an ecologically sustainable culture is a task that requires global cooperation
   (d)   a critical reevaluation of the "logic of growth" thesis is required
   (e)   all of the above

239

1. ____ The system composed of the interaction of all living organisms and their natural environment.
2. ____ The pattern by which environmental hazards are greatest in proximity to poor people and especially minorities.
3. ____ People living on a remote South Pacific island.
4. ____ The number of gallons of water consumed by a person in the U.S. over a lifetime.
5. ____ The study of the interaction of living organisms and the natural environment.
6. ____ The number of people added to the world's population each year (net gain).
7. ____ A religious minority living in Cairo who recycle solid waste throughout the city.
8. ____ The earth's surface and atmosphere, including living organisms as well as the air, soil, and other resources necessary to sustain life.
9. ____ Regions of dense forestation most of which circle the globe close to the equator.
10. ____ A situation in which our relationship with the environment, while yielding short-term benefits, generates negative long-term consequences.

a.	natural environment	f.	ecology
b.	Zebaleen	g.	environmental deficit
c.	10 million	h.	rain forests
d.	Nauruans	i.	environmental racism
e.	90 million	j.	ecosystem

Fill-In

1. The _____ _____ refers to the earth's surface and atmosphere, including living organisms, air, water, soil, and other resources necessary to sustain life.
2. An _____ is defined as the system composed of the interaction of all living organisms and their natural environment.
3. Sociology makes three vital contributions to ecological debates, including: exploring what the environment _____ to people of varying social backgrounds, monitoring the _____ on many environmental issues, and demonstrating how human _____ _____ put mounting stress on the natural environment.
4. The concept of *environmental deficit* implies three important ideas. First, the state of the environment is a _____ _____. Second, much environmental damage is _____. And third, in some respects environmental damage is _____.
5. Our planet suffers not just from economic underdevelopment in some regions, but also from economic _____ in others.
6. *Africa* has an annual population growth rate of _____ percent.
7. Core values that underlie cultural patterns in the U.S. include progress, material comfort, and science. Such values form the foundation for the _____ *thesis*.
8. The _____ *thesis* states that humanity must implement policies to control the growth of population, material production, and the use of resources in order to avoid environmental collapse.

9. It is estimated that fifty percent of *household trash* in the U.S. is _____.
10. _____ *percent* of our solid waste that is not burned or recycled "never goes away."
11. The earth naturally recycles water and refreshes the land through what scientists call the _____ cycle.
12. Two major concerns dominate discussion of *water* and the natural environment. The first is _____; the second is _____.
13. The _____ people of Cairo have amazed the world with their determination and ingenuity, turning one of the planet's foulest dumps into an efficient recycling center.
14. We need to curb *water consumption* by industry, which uses _____ percent of the global total, and by farming, which consumes _____ of the total for irrigation.
15. Experts estimate the atmospheric concentration of *carbon dioxide* is now _____ to _____ percent higher than it was 150 years ago.
16. _____ _____ is a theoretical paradigm that explores the relationship between human culture and the natural environment.
17. *Structural-functional* analysis is criticized for overlooking the issues of _____ and _____ and how these affect our relationship with the natural environment.
18. *Social-conflict theory* highlights the very issues that structural-functionalism tends to overlook: _____ and _____.
19. Strategies for creating an *ecologically sustainable culture* include _____, _____, and bringing _____ _____ under control.
20. _____ *percent* of U.S. adults would "accept a lower standard of living" to protect the environment.

Definition and Short-Answer

1. Differentiate between the concepts *ecology* and *natural environment*.
2. What three important ideas are implied by the concept *environmental deficit*?
3. Briefly describe the pattern of word *population growth* prior to an after the Industrial Revolution.
4. Critically differentiate between the *logic of growth* and the *limits to growth* views concerning the relationship between human technology and the natural environment.
5. What is meant by the term *disposable society*? What evidence is being presented to support this view of the U.S.?
6. Review the global research concerning either *water pollution* or *air pollution*.
7. Discuss the connection between the depletion of the rain forest and global warming and declining biodiversity.
8. Differentiate between the *structural-functional, cultural ecology,* and *social-conflict* views on the relationship between human society and the natural world. What are three important insights offered by each view? What is one criticism of each view?
9. What are the three strategies identified for creating an *ecologically sustainable culture*?
10. What are the fundamental changes in the ways we think about ourselves and the world which are being suggested in the text? What other changes in our thinking would you suggest be made?

PART VI: ANSWERS TO STUDY QUESTIONS

True-False

1.	T	(p. 399)	8.	F	(p. 406)
2.	T	(p. 401)	9.	T	(p. 406)
3.	T	(pp. 403-404)	10.	F	(p. 409)
4.	T	(p. 404)	11.	F	(p. 411)
5.	F	(p. 405)	12.	F	(p. 411)
6.	T	(p. 405)	13.	F	(p. 412)
7.	F	(p. 406)	14.	T	(p. 414)

Multiple-Choice

1.	d	(p. 399)	10.	b	(p. 406)
2.	c	(p. 400)	11.	e	(p. 409)
3.	a	(p. 400)	12.	b	(p. 411)
4.	e	(pp. 410-402)	13.	a	(p. 411)
5.	c	(p. 403)	14.	c	(p. 411)
6.	d	(pp. 403-404)	15.	d	(p. 412)
7.	e	(pp. 404-405)	16.	d	(p. 416)
8.	b	(p. 405)	17.	e	(p. 416)
9.	c	(p. 406)			

Matching

1.	j	(p. 400)	6.	e	(p. 401)
2.	i	(p. 414)	7.	b	(p. 407)
3.	d	(p. 399)	8.	a	(p. 399)
4.	c	(p. 409)	9.	h	(p. 411)
5.	f	(p. 399)	10.	g	(p. 401)

Fill-In

1. natural environment (p. 399)
2. ecosystem (p. 400)
3. means, public pulse, social patterns (p. 400)
4. social issue, unintended, reversible (p. 401)
5. overdevelopment (p. 403)
6. 2.5 (p. 403)
7. logic of growth (p. 403)
8. limits of growth (p. 404)
9. paper (p. 406)

10.   80 (p. 406)
11.   hydrological (p. 406)
12.   supply, pollution (p. 406)
13.   Zebaleen (p. 407)
14.   25, two-thirds (p. 411)
15.   20-30 (p. 411)
16.   Cultural ecology (p. 412)
17.   inequality, power (p. 412)
18.   power, inequality (p. 413)
19.   conservation, reducing waste, population growth (p. 4416)
20.   30.3 (p. 417)

PART VII: IN FOCUS—IMPORTANT ISSUES

- What are the three major roles sociology can play in the study of the *natural environment*?

- Describe each both of the following outlooks on environmental deficit.

    Logic of Growth Thesis:

    Limits to Growth Thesis:

- Make reference to two key points made in the text concerning each of the following *environmental issues*.

    Solid Waste:

    Preserving Clean Water:

    Clearing the Air:

    Acid Rain:

    The Rain Forests:

- Describe how each of the following *theories* help us see how the operation of society affects the natural environment.

  Structural-Functional Analysis:

  Cultural Ecology:

  Social-Conflict Analysis:

- *Sustainable living* call for three basic strategies. What are these?

- The above strategies will only work if we make three important *connections*. What are these?

PART VIII: ANALYSIS AND COMMENT

Global Sociology

"Turning the Tide: A Report from Egypt"

Key Points: Questions:

Critical Thinking

"Why Grandmother Had No Trash"

Key Points: Questions:

Controversy and Debate

"Reclaiming the Environment: What Are We Willing to Give Up?"

Key Points: Questions:

Window on the World--Global Map 15-1

"Water Consumption in Global Perspective"

Key Points: Questions:

Seeing Ourselves--National Map 15-1

"Air Pollution across the United States"

Key Points: Questions:

<table>
<tr><td>16</td><td></td></tr>
</table>

16 Social Change: Modern and Postmodern Societies

PART I: CHAPTER OUTLINE

I.   What is Social Change?
II.   Causes of Social Change
    A.   Culture and Change
    B.   Conflict and Change
    C.   Ideas and Change
    D.   Demographic Change
    E.   Social Movements and Change
III.   Modernity
    A.   Ferdinand Tonnies: The Loss of Community
    B.   Emile Durkheim: The Division of Labor
    C.   Max Weber: Rationalization
    D.   Karl Marx: Capitalism
IV.   Structural-Functional Analysis: The Theory of Mass Society
    A.   The Mass Scale of Modern Life
    B.   The Ever-expanding State
V.   Social Conflict Analysis: The Theory of Class Society
    A.   Capitalism
    B.   Persistent Inequality
VI.   Modernity and the Individual
    A.   Mass Society: Problems of Identity
    B.   Class Society: Problems of Powerlessness
VII.   Modernity and Progress
    A.   Modernity and Global Variation
VIII.   Postmodernity
IX.   Looking Ahead: Modernization and Our Global Future
X.   Summary
XI.   Key Concepts
XII: Critical-Thinking Questions
XIII.   Learning Exercises

PART II: LEARNING OBJECTIVES

1. To be able to identify and describe the four general characteristics of social change.
2. To be able to identify and illustrate the different sources of social change.
3. To be able to identify and describe the four basic types of social movements
4. To be able to identify and describe the four different theories used to understand social movements.
5. To be able to identify and provide illustrations for each of the four stages of a social movement.
6. To be able to discuss the views on social change as offered by Ferdinand Tonnies, Emile Durkheim, Max Weber, and Karl Marx.
7. To be able to identify and describe the general characteristics of modernization.
8. To be able to identify the key ideas of two major interpretations of modern society: mass society and class society.
9. To be able to discuss the ideas of postmodernist thinkers and critically consider their relevance for our society.

PART III: KEY CONCEPTS

anomie
class society
diffusion
discovery
division of labor
Gemeinschaft
Gesellschaft
individualism
invention
mass society
mechanical solidarity
modernity
modernization
organic solidarity
other-directedness
Postmodernity
progress
relative deprivation
social change
social character
social movement
tradition-directedness

PART IV: IMPORTANT RESEARCHERS

Karl Marx   Max Weber

Emile Durkheim   Ferdinand Toennies

David Reisman   Herbert Marcuse

PART V: STUDY QUESTIONS

True-False

1. T F Three pivotal *sources* of social change are *diffusion, invention,* and *discovery*.
2. T F *Max Weber* argued that technology and conflict are more important than ideas in transforming society.
3. T F Overall, only about 9 percent of U.S. residents have not moved during the last thirty years.
4. T F *Reformative social movements* have greater focus and less scope than *redemptive social movements*.
5. T F A major weakness of *new social movements* is that they fail to take into consideration "quality-of-life issues."
6. T F Using *mass-society theory*, social movements are viewed as being both personal and political.
7. T F *Mass-society theory* suggests that social movements attract socially isolated people who feel personally insignificant.
8. T F *Resource-mobilization theory* suggests that "discontent" is the most significant resource in determining the success of a social movement.

9.	T	F	*Coalescence* follows *bureaucratization* as a stage in the development of a social movement.
10.	T	F	According to *Peter Berger*, a characteristic of modernization is the expression of individual choice.
11.	T	F	*Modernity* is defined as social patterns linked to industrialization.
12.	T	F	The concepts of *Gemeinschaft* and *Gesellschaft* were developed by *Ferdinand Tonnies*.
13.	T	F	According to our author, *Emile Durkheim's* view of modernity is more optimistic than that of *Ferdinand Tonnies*.
14.	T	F	Emile Durkheim considered the suicide rate to be a good index of *anomie*.
15.	T	F	Compared to *Emile Durkheim and* Ferdinand Tonnies, *Max Weber* was more critical of modern society, believing that the rationalization of bureaucracies would cause people to become alienated.
16.	T	F	*Max Weber* believed that rational thinking was disappearing as modern society emerged from traditional society.
17.	T	F	For *Karl Marx*, modern society was synonymous with *capitalism*.
18.	T	F	A *mass society* is one in which industry and bureaucracy have eroded traditional social ties.
19.	T	F	A *class society* is a capitalist society with pronounced social stratification.
20.	T	F	According to *David Reisman*, a type of social character he labels *other-directedness* represents small, traditional societies.
21.	T	F	According to *class-society theory*, the effects of modernization include the reduction of capitalist economies and an increase in social equality.
22.	T	F	People in the U.S. are less likely than people in other industrialized societies to see *scientific advances* as helpful for humanity.
23.	T	F	*Postmodernity* refers to the recent trend in industrialized societies of a return to traditional values and practices.
24.	T	F	The *communitarian movement* rests on the premise that strong rights presume strong responsibilities.

Multiple-Choice

1. The *Kaiapo*:

   (a) is a small society in Brazil.
   (b) is a ritual among the Mbuti of the Ituri forest.
   (c) is a sacred tradition involving animal sacrifices which has been made illegal by the Canadian government.
   (d) are a people of Asia who represent the Gesellschaft concept developed by Ferdinand Tonnies.
   (e) is a ritualistic war pattern of the Maring, a New Guinea culture of horticulturalists.

249

2.   _____ refers to the transformation of culture and social institutions over time.

   (a)   Social change
   (b)   Cultural lag
   (c)   Modernization
   (d)   Anomie
   (c)   Rationalization

3.   The movement of people, ideas, and products from one society to another is known as:

   (a)   anomie.
   (b)   Discovery.
   (c)   Diffusion.
   (d)   cultural lag.
   (e)   cultural relativism.

4.   According to the author, which type of *social movement* is least threatening to the status quo because it seeks limited change in only some part of the population?

   (a)   revolutionary
   (b)   alternative
   (c)   deprivation
   (d)   redemptive

5.   What type of social movement seeks limited social change for the entire society?

   (a)   revolutionary
   (b)   redemptive
   (c)   deprivation
   (d)   alternative
   (e)   reformative

6.   _____ *theory* suggests social movements attract socially isolated people who feel personally insignificant.

   (a)   Mass-society
   (b)   Structural-strain
   (c)   Resource-mobilization
   (d)   New social movements

7. *Emergence* is identified as stage one of a social movement. Which of the following is *not* identified as a stage in the evolution of a social movement?

    (a) bureaucratization
    (b) coalescence
    (c) decline
    (d) realignment

8. _____ is the process of social change initiated by industrialization.

    (a) Postmodernity
    (b) Anomie
    (c) Mass society
    (d) Modernization
    (e) Modernity

9. For *Emile Durkheim*, modernization is defined by the increasing _____ of a society.

    (a) mechanical solidarity
    (b) alienation
    (c) division of labor
    (d) conspicuous consumption

10. For *Max Weber*, modernity means replacing a traditional world with a _____ way of thinking.

    (a) alienated
    (b) marginal
    (c) mechanical
    (d) organic
    (e) rational

11. *Emile Durkheim's* concepts of *mechanical solidarity* and *organic solidarity* are similar in meaning to the concepts:

    (a) mass society and class society.
    (b) tradition-directedness and other-directedness.
    (c) anomie and progress.
    (d) Gemeinschaft and Gesellschaft.
    (e) none of the above

12. Which of the following is most *accurate*:

    (a) Emile Durkheim's concept of organic solidarity refers to social bonds of mutual dependency based on specialization
    (b) Ferdinand Tonnies saw societies as changing from the social organization based on Gesellschaft to the social organization based on Gemeinschaft
    (c) Peter Berger argued that modern society offers less autonomy than is found in preindustrial societies
    (d) Emile Durkheim's concept of mechanical solidarity is very similar in meaning to Ferdinand Tonnies' concept of Gesellschaft

13. According to *Karl Marx*, modern society was synonymous with _____.

    (a) equality.
    (b) rationality.
    (c) community.
    (d) bureaucracy.
    (e) capitalism.

14. _____ *theory* focuses on the expanding scale of social life and the rise of the state in the study of modernization.

    (a) Dependency
    (b) Modernization
    (c) Social class
    (d) Rationalization
    (e) Mass society

15. _____ *theory* maintains that persistent inequality undermines modern society's promise of individual freedom.

    (a) Mass-society
    (b) Class-society
    (c) Mechanical-society
    (d) Traditional-society

16. Which social scientist described *modernization* in terms of its affects on *social character*?

    (a) Peter Berger
    (b) William Ogburn
    (c) David Reisman
    (d) Herbet Marcuse
    (e) David Klein

17. _____ suggested that we be critical of *Max Weber's* view that modern society is rational because technological advances rarely empower people; instead, we should focus on the issue of how technology tends to reduce people's control over their own lives.

    (a)   Emile Durkheim
    (b)   Herbert Spencer
    (c)   David Reisman
    (d)   Herbert Marcuse
    (e)   Ferdinand Tonnies

18. According to public opinion polls, in which of the following modern societies does the largest percentage of the population believe that *scientific advances* are helping humanity?

    (a)   Great Britain
    (b)   Japan
    (c)   The United States
    (d)   Canada
    (e)   Mexico

19. The bright light of "progress" is fading; science no longer holds the answers; cultural debates are intensifying; in important respects, modernity has failed; and social institutions are changing--are all themes running through _____ *thinking*.

    (a)   class society
    (b)   postmodern
    (c)   mass society
    (d)   social movements

20. According to *dependency theory*:

    (a)   today's poor societies have little ability to modernize, even if they want to.
    (b)   The major barrier to economic development is not traditionalism but global domination.
    (c)   Rich nations achieved their modernization at the expense of poor ones.
    (d)   Continuing ties with rich societies will only perpetuate current patterns of global inequality.
    (e)   All of the above.

Matching

1. ___ A social movement with selective focus, but seeking radical change in some individuals.
2. ___ The premise that strong rights presume strong responsibilities.
3. ___ Social patterns linked to industrialization.
4. ___ He developed of *Gemeinschaft* and *Gesellschaft*.
5. ___ The transformation of culture and social institutions over time.
6. ___ Organized efforts to encourage or oppose some dimension of change.
7. ___ He developed the concepts of *mechanical* and *organic solidarity*.
8. ___ A society in which industry and bureaucracy have eroded traditional social ties.
9. ___ He argues that the primary values of any society are set not by government but by people living in communities and, especially, by families raising their children.
10. ___ A theory that suggests social movements attract socially isolated people who seek, through their membership, a sense of identity and purpose.
11. ___ A theory claiming that in the past the entire world was poor and that technological change, especially the Industrial Revolution, enhanced human productivity and raised living standards.
12. ___ The *third stage* of a social movement.
13. ___ A receptiveness to the latest trends and fashions, often evident in the practice of imitating others.
14. ___ A condition in which society provides little moral guidance to individuals.
15. ___ Social patterns characteristic of a *postindustrial society*.
16. ___ Specialized economic activity.
17. ___ A capitalist society with pronounced social stratification.
18. ___ Social movements aiming for limited change, but targeting everyone.

a.	social movements	g.	bureaucratization	m.	reformative
b.	social change	h.	division of labor	n.	postmodernity
c.	class society	i.	redemptive	o.	Emile Durkheim
d.	other-directedness	j.	anomie	p.	William Bennet
e.	mass-society theory	k.	modernity	q.	communitarianism
f.	mass-society	l.	modernization theory	r.	Ferdinand Tonnies

Fill-In

1. _____ refers to the transformation of culture and social institutions over time.
2. Focusing on culture as a source, *social change* results from three basic processes: _____, _____, and _____.
3. _____ _____ *theory* points out that no social movement is likely to succeed—or even get off the ground—without substantial resources.
4. The *third stage* of a social movement after emergence and coalescence is _____.
5. _____ refers to patterns of social life linked to industrialization.
6. *Emile Durkheim's* concept of *organic solidarity* is closely related to *Ferdinand Tonnies'* concept of _____.

7. _____ is a condition in which society provides little moral guidance to individuals.

8. For *Max Weber*, modernity amounts to the progressive replacement of a traditional world-view with a _____ way of thinking.

9. *Mass society theory* draws upon the ideas of _____, _____, and _____.

10. _____ *society* is a capitalist society with pronounced social stratification.

11. _____ _____ refers to personality patterns common to members of a society.

12. *David Reisman* argues that preindustrial societies promote _____, or rigid personalities based on conformity to time-honored ways of living.

13. Five themes have emerged as part of *postmodern thinking*. These include that in important respects, _____ has failed; The bright promise of "_____" is fading; _____ no longer holds the answers; Cultural debates are fading; And, social institutions are _____.

14. In the *Critical Thinking* box concerning the question of whether the U.S. is a nation in decline, from William Bennet's point of view, the primary _____ of any society are not set by _____ but by _____ living in communities and, especially, by _____ raising their children.

Definition and Short-Answer

1. What are four characteristics of *social change*?

2. Five general domains which are involved in *causing* social change are identified and discussed in the text. List these and provide an example for each.

3. *Peter Berger* identifies four general characteristics of *modern societies*. What are these characteristics?

4. Differentiate between *Ferdinand Tonnies, Emile Durkheim, Max Weber,* and *Karl Marx's* perspective on modernization.

5. What factors of *modernization* do theorists operating from the *mass society* theory focus upon?

6. What factors of *modernization* do theorists operating from the *mass society* theory focus upon?

7. What are the two types of *social character* identified by *David Reisman*? Define each of these.

8. What are the arguments being made by *postmodernists* concerning social change in modern society? What do critics of this view say?

9. Referring to *Table 16-1*, select a nonindustrialized society and compare it to the U.S. on four elements of society identified in the table. Provide a specific illustration representing a relative comparison for each element.

10. Four general types of *social movements* are discussed in the text. Identify, define, and illustrate each of these.

11. Four explanations of *social movements* are discussed in the text. Identify and describe each of these.

12. *Peter Berger* has identified four major characteristics of modernization. What are these? Provide an illustration for each of these.

PART VII: ANSWERS TO STUDY QUESTIONS

True-False

1.	T	(p. 424)	13.	T	(p. 429)
2.	F	(pp. 424-425)	14.	T	(p. 429)
3.	T	(p. 424)	15.	T	(p. 429)
4.	F	(p. 425)	16.	F	(p. 429)
5.	F	(p. 426)	17.	T	(p. 430)
6.	T	(p. 426)	18.	T	(p. 431)
7.	T	(p. 426)	19.	T	(p. 433)
8.	F	(p. 426)	20.	F	(pp. 434-435)
9.	F	(p. 427)	21.	F	(p. 434)
10.	T	(p. 427)	22.	F	(p. 436)
11.	T	(p. 427)	23.	F	(p. 437)
12.	T	(p. 428)	24.	T	(p. 441)

Multiple Choice

1.	a	(p. 421)	11.	d	(p. 429)
2.	c	(p. 422)	12.	a	(p. 429)
3.	b	(p. 424)	13.	e	(p. 430)
4.	b	(p. 425)	14.	e	(pp. 432-434)
5.	e	(p. 425)	15.	b	(p. 433)
6.	a	(p. 417)	16.	c	(p. 434)
7.	d	(pp. 426-427)	17.	d	(p. 436)
8.	d	(p. 427)	18.	c	(p. 436)
9.	c	(p. 429)	19.	b	(pp. 438-439)
10.	e	(p. 429)	20.	e	(pp. 439-440)

Matching

1.	i	(p. 425)	10.	e	(p. 426)
2.	q	(p. 441)	11.	l	(p. 439)
3.	k	(p. 427)	12.	g	(p. 427)
4.	r	(p. 428)	13.	d	(p. 435)
5.	b	(p. 422)	14.	j	(p. 429)
6.	a	(p. 425)	15.	n	(p. 437)
7.	o	(p. 429)	16.	h	(p. 429)
8.	f	(p. 431)	17.	c	(p. 433)
9.	p	(p. 438)	18.	m	(p. 425)

Fill-In

1.   social change (p. 422)
2.   invention, discovery, diffusion (p. 424)
3.   Resource mobilization (p. 426)
4.   bureaucratization (p. 427)
5.   modernity (p. 427)
6.   Gesellschaft (p. 428)
7.   anomie (p. 429)
8.   rational (p. 429)
9.   Tonnies, Durkheim, Weber (p. 431)
10.   class (p. 433)
11.   social character (p. 434)
12.   tradition-directedness (p. 434)
13.   modernity, progress, science, intensifying, changing (pp. 438-439)
14.   values, government, people, families (p. 438)

PART VII: IN FOCUS—IMPORTANT ISSUES

- What are the four major characteristics of *social change?*

- Provide an illustration for each of the following major *causes of social change.*

    Culture and change:

    Conflict and change:

    Ideas and change:

    Demographic change:

    Social movements and change:

- Provide an illustration for each of the following *types of social movements.*

  Alternative:

  Redemptive:

  Reformative:

  Revolutionary:

- What points do each of the following theories make about *understanding social movements?*

  Relative deprivation:

  Mass-society:

  Resource-mobilization:

  New social movements:

- According to *Peter Berger*, what are the four major *characteristics of modernity?*

- Describe modern society from the point of view of each of the following theoriests.

  Ferdinand Tonnies:

  Emile Durkheim:

  Max Weber:

  Karl Marx:

- What do structural-functionalists mean by *mass society*?

- What do social-conflict theorists mean by *class society?*

- What are the major themes of *postmodern thinking?*

PART VIII: COMMENT AND ANALYSIS

Critical Thinking

"The United States: A Nation in Decline?"

Key Points: Questions:

Controversy and Debate

"Personal Freedom and Social Responsibility: Can We Have It Both Ways?"

Key Points: Questions:

Seeing Ourselves--National Map 16-1

"Who Stays Put? Residential Stability across the United States"

Key Points: Questions: